A WORLD
without
BARRIERS

God bless you BroCollins

Joy P. Mall

specially-abled@gmail.com

Published by:
Mall Publishing Company
12693 Cold Springs Drive
Huntley, Illinois 60142
877-203-2453
info@mallpublishing.biz
www.mallpublishing.biz

Cover and text design by Marlon Villadiego

ISBN 1-934165-51-4

For licensing / copyright information, for additional copies or for use in specialized settings contact:

Joy P. Mall
Empowering the Specially Abled International
4235 N. Kedvale Avenue, Suite 1A
Chicago, Illinois 60641
Email: specially.abled@gmail.com

A WORLD *without* BARRIERS

**Providing Doors of Opportunity
to Persons with Disabilities in India**

JOY P. MALL

Mall Publishing Co.

THE PRINTED WORD THE PLANTED SEED

HUNTLEY, ILLINOIS

Table of Contents

Dedication

To my parents Victoria and Emanuel Mall who spent their lives in India, serving and ministering with love and compassion to the needy and marginalized. Their unwavering faith and passion to serve the helpless gave me hope and strength to never give up my quest for personal freedom that transcends all barriers.

I hope my story will empower everyone with disability to be inspired and continue the quest for your own personal freedom that knows no barrier.

Endorsements

Joy Mall has vividly described conditions in India for persons with disabilities, highlighting the role of partnerships and providing abundant references and agency descriptions. Even more importantly, Joy's story provides overwhelming testimony to the abundant power of God in using one life (one earthen vessel) committed to Him-- even today Christ multiplies loaves and fishes to do abundantly more than we could ever ask or imagine.

This narrative of hope and inspiration testifies to the difference that even a small change can make--if we cannot change the world, we can be committed to Christ, we can have compassion for our neighbor, and we can change the height of a sink! I would recommend this insightful work for anyone interested in outreach among the disabled, especially in the international context.

Janet G. Metzger, Ph.D.
Professor of Intercultural Studies,
Johnson University, Knoxville, TN

Joy officially entered our MS program in the fall of 2006. In the years since, I have come to know her as an instructor for some of her coursework, as an academic advisor, and as her thesis advisor. In this latter capacity we had many long but ultimately indeterminate discussions over possible studies that she could conduct to fulfill the requirements for the degree. Nothing seemed quite right. And there were those periodic absences from the program, where Joy would travel to India as part of her "non-academic" life. I thought she would never finish the degree.

Then in 2009 she invited me to a presentation that she was doing that was part of this "other" life. She was raising funds for another trip, describing what she did as part of these travels to India: the effort to inspire those among the most marginalized, to change the attitudes of those who marginalize, and to affect a society and system one person and one structure at a time. I was deeply touched. Joy did not need to conduct a study. Joy needed to do more in this "other" life.

Thus, this story of her work in India in 2010. It is driven and deeply inspired and informed by her religious faith. In these pages one has the opportunity to peer over her shoulder during her travels and experience another culture through the eyes of one who is both an insider and alien to her community and society. In many ways it is a universal story of disablement. And while religion and disability has had a difficult and often controversial connection, Joy's message here is one of hope, strength, and a vision of a better future based on respect and the fundamental value of all lives.

Glenn T Fujiura, PhD
Interim Dean, College of Applied Health Sciences
University of Illinois at Chicago

Acknowledgments

First and foremost, I am grateful to the Lord Jesus Christ for giving me life, life eternal. God has allowed me to live with a disability which has given me insight into the needs of the disability community. My vision is to serve this forgotten group of people and their families. My goal is to pass along this vision to others in India and the world at large.

I am grateful to Joni and Friends, Operation Equip India, my home church Harvest Christian Center and other churches in the United States and India for the privilege of working under their umbrella in order to serve the disability community and encourage others to do the same. I am thankful for the blessing of all their prayers. I also want to express my appreciation for those who financially supported my 2010 trip to India.

I am thankful to Karen Aukland and her continued support as a travel and ministry partner, as well as her help in organizing the trip, teaching, and presentation material. A special thanks to Dr. Janet Metzger for standing with me through this long journey through her prayer support, her wise counsel and countless other ways too numerous to mention. Also, to Urban Resources/Chicago for the scholarship and grant-in-aid that allowed me to fulfill my dream.

To Carolyn Johnson and Crystal Anderson for hours spent condensing hundreds of pages of material typing and retyping the paper and especially for their patience. To my friend and ministry advisor Susan Ostrum, profound thanks for the hours spent editing the final project. Also, to all of my personal assistants who faithfully served and helped to keep my life and house organized so I would not go insane. Likewise to my brother Ted for time spent formatting and making this project both attractive and professional.

To Emma and Wil Das (sister and brother in law) thank you for loving me, listening to me, upholding me and being my advocate through this long and often difficult adventure.

Many thanks to Donna Mall (sister-in-law) for being the support I needed to complete the last leg of the project through prayers, reading, and helping shape the narrative in words and ways I wanted to express. And to both Ernest (my brother) and Donna, thank you for equipping me to share my vision with others by publishing my journey of love.

Last but not least, Professor Glenn Fujiura. Over the last seven years you have been my mentor, advisor, supporter, cheerleader and have become a friend. Thank you for believing in me and inspiring me to grab hold of my dream to empower others, and thus change the world one person at a time.

About the Author

Joy Mall considers herself a living miracle. When she was four months old she contracted Poliomyelitis and was given no hope of survival. Defying all odds, she did survive by the grace of God. However she was never able to walk.

In 1975 she relocated to the U.S from India. Shortly after her arrival she developed a desire to become both a voice and a resource for the marginalized in the disability community in the U.S, India and South Asia.

Her goal is to raise disability awareness in the U.S and abroad. Joy serves as a ministry associate of Joni and Friends International. Here she regularly serves at Family Retreat and Wheels for the World. Her role is to minister to families with disability, distribute wheelchairs and share God's love in developing countries. Joy has been an intrinsic part of South Asian Friendship Center where she helped develop and oversee the ESL and Disability Program. While there, she helped train volunteers and minister to women and families in difficult circumstances.

Armed with a Bachelor of Arts in Psychology and a Master of Arts in

Disabilities and Human Developments, Joy travels into the small unnoticed villages in India. Her love and devotion to those without hope is a testimony to God's love and man's determination. Her desire is to spur others to help open up doors of opportunity to those who have limited hope for a future.

Her words are both inspirational and convicting. "Everyone faces limitations in the course of a lifetime. However life is a series of choices and one can either face the personal challenge directly or allow it to restrict their potential. In my life, I refuse to allow my disability to be the barrier that determines my future. So join with me and embrace my vision of A World Without Barriers".

Foreword

Before You Begin...

I've gotten used to being on display. Whether it's the child studying my wheelchair or the waiter eyeing me carefully as I use my bent spoon to eat a meal, I'm aware that people are watching. Some might watch out of pity, some out of admiration. I sense that all watch with curiosity. It comes with a disability.

It's what Joy Mall faces everyday. Like Joy, I choose to think that people are curious for good reasons. That's because followers of Jesus Christ are constrained to think the best of others. We are called to be on display – all for the benefit of building others up in the faith. God's Word tells us to smile from the inside-out as his grace shows up through our physical limitations. When people eye Joy Mall, sitting in her wheelchair, smiling, I believe they are thinking, How great her God must be to inspire such faith and confidence.

Somehow, I don't think Joy minds being on display. Her story inspires all who observe her. I remember meeting her many years ago during a visit to Chicago. A local church was sponsoring a carnival street-fair – and Joy was sitting there, dressed up like a clown and welcoming everyone! I thought, here's a woman with a disability who's got a great self-image, a wonderful attitude toward life, and an interest in reaching out to others. It's all the more fun when you think that this is the same woman who just graduated from the University of Chicago with a Master's of Science in Disability and Human Development!

Joy Mall is going somewhere with her Master's degree and her love for the Lord Jesus. I have prayed for her during her many ministry trips to India, the land of her heritage. Once when Joy broke her ankle on a trip, everyone thought she would stay back at the hotel – not Joy; she was back in her wheelchair in no time, serving and sharing. Joy has a great heart for reaching people with disabilities in that land of over 1 billion people.

Yes, she is going somewhere. In a world that is splitting apart at the seams, we need to hear from courageous people who love extending the grace of God through their stories of hope and healing. My friend Joy does that... and more. On the following pages, you will discover a woman who is very ordinary, yet extraordinary. And like me, you will think, If Joy Mall can overcome her limitations with God's grace, I can, too.

Joni Eareckson Tada
Joni and Friends International Disability Center
Agoura Hills, California

Abstract

The following account describes my experiences during a 2010 trip to India that was conducted as part of an MS project. It is written in narrative form and contains stories and pictures which clarify the objective of the project. My purpose is to encourage people with disabilities to build their self esteem by becoming independent, and in turn, train others with disabilities to do the same. The objectives and goals of this project were accomplished by providing disability training in partnership with pastors, church leaders, medical professionals, social workers, community workers, disability groups, and people with disabilities and their families. The end result of each training session, which occurred in various cities in India, is summarized at the end of each chapter.

1

Preface

For many years, people with disabilities in India were a forgotten class. They were often shunned, because many Indians believe disabilities are the result of a curse, bad karma, witchcraft, or even punishment for sins. Children with disabilities were the most vulnerable, often experiencing neglect, malnutrition, teasing, and were considered a burden both to their families and to society. Children with Disabilities and adults were often abused by their relatives who were rarely confronted or punished for their actions. Prejudice even extended to the playgrounds, where able-bodied children were discouraged from playing with children with disabilities, because parents feared their child would somehow be negatively affected.

http://www.ucl.ac.uk/lc-ccr/lccstaff/raymond-lang/understanding_disability_in_india.pdf

http://sancd.org/uploads/pdf/disability.pdf

http://www.disabilityworld.org/04-05_03/violence/horrorstory.shtml

Schools in India were not willing to even consider taking children with disabilities. Having these children in the classroom would be disruptive to the other students, especially if the child with a disability needed assistance using the bathroom, feeding himself, or had difficulty communicating. The fact that a child had the cognitive ability to understand and express himself did not matter. The physical limitations of the student's disability were the only determining factor for admittance into the school system. For this reason, many parents of children with disabilities stopped pursuing an education for them.

I experienced firsthand the life of disability in India, when at four months of age, I was diagnosed with poliomyelitis. I was fortunate that I did not experience the emotional trauma of most children with disabilities, primarily because I was born into a loving Christian family. My father was a pastor and my mother was a missionary. Both were very protective of me, but they also wanted to provide me an opportunity for a normal life, as much as possible. However, there were some obstacles, literally. Many of the homes, both then and now, had architectural features, such as high thresholds and narrow doorways and steps, which made it difficult for me to get around.

In 1995, India passed the "Persons with Disabilities Act," a first of its kind legislation to ensure equal rights for people with disabilities. This legislation pertained to most of India, except for the states of Jammu and Kashmir. It empowers persons with disabilities by providing them with equal opportunities, ensuring equal rights, and protecting them against discrimination in education and employment. Included disabilities in this Act are blindness, low vision, leprosy-cured, hearing impairment, motor disabilities, mental retardation, and mental illness. Some of the benefits provided under this legislation include special schools equipped with vocational training facilities for children with disabilities; housing opportunities, the establishment of factories by entrepreneurs with disabilities, recreation centers, and insuring that three percent of all government jobs are reserved for adults with disabilities. Government funding is provided to Panchayats, village governments made up of five officials who make decisions regarding local politics and for building roads, schools, and public ramps which assist persons with disabilities (Disability India Network, 2006). (http://www.disabilityindia.org/pwdacts.cfm#ch5)

Three other laws focused on empowering the disabled: The Mental Health Act of 1987, The Rehabilitation Council of India Act 1992, and the National Trust for Welfare of Persons with Autism, Cerebral Palsy, Mental Retardation, and Multiple Disabilities Act of 1999. In addition, there are also medical corrections available through surgery and rehabilitation. At present, many families impacted by disabilities still are not aware of the programs available to them by the Indian government. For instance, many communities still do not take advantage of government funding to help make buildings accessible. And some do not know what medical and financial options are available to citizens with disabilities. Additionally, local superstitions and long held prejudicial attitudes toward persons with disabilities still exist. The social stigmas placed on individuals with disabilities in India are significantly different than the social barriers faced by Americans with disabilities. http://www.disabled-world.com/news/asia/india/

Background

In the summer of 2000, I attended a family retreat for people with disabilities, organized by Joni and Friends (JAF). Joni and Friends, a non-profit Christian organization, was founded by Joni Eareckson Tada who became a quadriplegic as a teenager, the result of a diving accident. Joni has been an advocate for people with disabilities for over 30 years. The vision of JAF is to energize and equip churches worldwide to reach those affected by disability through disability awareness and training sessions to help persons with disabilities use their leadership gifts and other gifts to serve their communities (Joni and Friends, 2011).

Summer, 2000 was my first experience at one of the JAF retreats. I had a great time spiritually and socially through participating in accessible activities such as horseback riding and boating. I can express the experience

JAF retreat: Llama trying to give me a kiss

Possibilities for wheelchair users

of that week in one sentence: "We were treated like royalty." The entire experience piqued my curiosity as to how JAF organized these retreats with such quality, intentionality, and care. The following year, I became a retreat volunteer with Joni and Friends. I was determined to learn from JAF everything I could about educating, equipping, and training others about disability issues. It was at that point that I started working with JAF.

In 2005, I began traveling with Wheels for the World (WFTW), a JAF ministry that collects and refurbishes donated wheelchairs, walkers, and crutches from adults and children in the U.S. and makes them available

Joy praying for recipients of wheelchairs

free of charge worldwide to persons with disabilities who cannot afford them (Joni and Friends, 2011). It was in that year that I traveled to India with WFTW for the first time. While there, I counseled with the families who received a wheelchair, walker or crutches. I encouraged the parents that

it is critical to treat their children, both with and without disabilities, the same, to invest time and effort into their child with disability to maximize his/her learning, and to view their children with potential to be educated and employed. Additionally, I counseled the families to allow the person with disability to do as much as possible for himself/herself to lead to optimal independence. The children and young people were encouraged to pursue their education, in spite of the difficulties they may encounter in school, and with perseverance, their parents and family members would more likely invest in their education. The young people were also encouraged to accomplish as much as they could, even if it took longer to complete the task. At the end of this chapter, there are a few stories included from the counseling sessions to illustrate how we, as a team, were able to help the people who came for mobility devices. The reason WFTW became dear to my heart was because of my own experience of receiving my first wheelchair when I was in 8th grade, from

Counseling a pre-med student who just received her first wheelchair at WFTW

a missionary who was a family friend. At that time, I was on the receiving end, but now working with WFTW, I witness that same excitement and happiness on the faces of other people with disabilities when receiving a wheelchair for the first time, knowing that their wheelchairs would provide them the same independence as it did for me. I would travel with WFTW again in 2006, 2007 and 2009 to deliver wheelchairs, counsel families, and advocate for disability awareness with local pastors and church leaders. Below are a few stories in which, through personal experience, encouragement, advice and counsel was given.

Shamsi: A Double Amputee

Shamsi, in her twenties and a double amputee, received a new wheelchair. She was brought to my counseling booth. I knew by her name that she was a Muslim woman. She told me her story.

"Eight months ago, I married and went to live with my husband and his family. A few days later, we went on an outing with his family. We had to cross railroad tracks. As we were walking, I kept lagging behind because, as a new bride, I was wearing a long veil. A train was coming, and the others crossed the tracks safely, but I tripped and fell. I couldn't get up, so I tried to crawl off the tracks. My clothes got caught and the train ran over me. I was in excruciating

Joy's first wheelchair

5

pain and passed out after seeing that part of my one leg was cut off and the other one was badly crushed. The doctor had to amputate my crushed leg. My parents brought me home from the hospital and have been taking care of me since the accident. My husband came to see me once in the hospital, but I don't have contact with him anymore."

I told her of Jesus' miracles and power that is taught in the Bible and reminded her it is also mentioned in the Quran. I shared part of my story, describing how Jesus Christ has given me strength all through my life. She shared about her fear and depression. I encouraged her, though there would be difficulties, that it is worth the effort to become as independent as possible.

Earlier, one of the Physical Therapists had mentioned to me that Shamsi needed to learn how to use a transfer board. She said she could not use it because she was afraid. Bringing Shamsi to the middle of the room, I demonstrated how I used it. With each move, I called upon the name of Jesus to emphasize that there is power in the Name of Jesus. Then I asked Shamsi to do the same. She began moving very slowly and saying the name of Jesus after every breath. She transferred herself from her wheelchair to the chair, broadly smiling, and then transferred back to her wheelchair. She truly had a look of accomplishment.

Katie

I met Katie in India in 2006, when her dad brought her to receive a wheelchair. After receiving her new wheelchair, Katie and her dad came to my booth. I waved and smiled at Katie. Though she gave me a weak smile, she waved at me with much effort. She was tired, having already been at the distribution center for at least three hours and having traveled a great distance to come to the site.

Katie appeared to be about three years old, but when I asked how old she was, her father informed me she was six years old. When I asked what Katie's diagnosis was, he said, "We don't have a diagnosis, because we never took her to a doctor." It broke my heart that she was six years old and had

Katie, 2006

never seen a doctor. I asked the father "Do you have other children and do they have any kind of disabilities?" He answered, "No, the other two children are fine," and then he started telling me about how intelligent they were and what good grades they get. I could tell he was very proud of them. When asked what he would do if one of his other children got sick, he replied, "Oh, I will take them to the doctor." I asked, "Then why did you not take Katie to the doctor? Is she less important to you?" He replied, "No, I love her very much, no different than the other two children, and that is why I brought her to you so she could have a wheelchair." When I asked, "Then why did you never take her to the doctor?" Katie's father answered that family and friends said she wouldn't live and she would not get better, so it would not be worth investing in doctors for her. I shared with him that God views Katie as His creation and values her, suggesting that when he chose not to take Katie to the doctor, he was treating her differently. "I know Christ died for me and for Katie, as well as for you, and because of this **we** do not have the right to treat her differently than anyone else." With tears rolling down his cheeks, he said, "No one ever talked to me like this, Madam, I promise you I will take Katie to the doctor and pray for her in the name of Jesus like you did."

John and Mary

A couple, John and Mary, came to the Counseling Booth at the Wheels Distribution in India. John is a mechanical engineer by profession. Eight months earlier, he had fallen, hurting the lower part of his spine and paralyzing him from the waist down. Due to the disability, he was unable to work, and therefore, was feeling less of a husband and provider for his family. Consequently, he was fighting depression. I shared God's encouragement with John and Mary, explaining how our suffering is nothing compared to what Jesus suffered for us. As tears started to roll down John's cheeks and I continued to share with him, I noticed his expression of depression slowly disappeared. I encouraged them and prayed with them.

I taught John how to use his new transfer board, sharing with him that by being able to use the board, he would become more independent. With each successful transfer, he smiled. As I continued to encourage John, he began to cry. Reaching over, Mary wiped his tears, consoling him, "Everything will be fine and don't cry." Explaining to both of them that it is okay for

John and Mary

John to cry and grieve, as he had lived independently all these years and now has lost that ability, I said, "John, many times you are going to feel that you are not good enough, but our disability doesn't determine that, it is our character that does. With or without disability, you are a man, a husband, an engineer, a skilled man—that's something nobody can change. At times you will feel that you are less of a man and a husband sexually or you may think you wife feels that way, but love for our spouses is not determined by our sexuality. It is determined by how we choose to love, care and respect them. So you continue to love your wife, appreciate her for her love and all she does for you. That is all she is expecting from you." Sobbing, John shared, "I have never said these things to anybody. I am surprised that you understand how I feel." Mary gave me a hug, whispering to me that she had never cried in front of John since the accident. Explaining that John's disability is a loss to both of them, I encouraged Mary in her need to grieve over the loss of his independence. They just needed to remember that disability is not the end of the world, and with each other's and God's help, they can still be a happy couple, in spite of some limitations, They can be independent and move forward. They expressed the desire to read Joni's (Joni Eareckson Tada) biography and the Bible, so we gave those books as a gift to them. They left with a grateful heart for all the help and encouragement.

It was through JAF/WFTW that I learned about Operation Equip India (OEI), an affiliate organization of JAF in India. OEI is dedicated to reaching persons with disability in all of India by providing education, vocational training, job placement assistance, corrective surgeries, and physical therapy for their clients as they are accepted for one or more of these services. In 2008, I was invited to India by OEI to assist in providing disability training for churches in four districts in the state of Northern Karnataka. Again in 2009, I spoke in three other districts in that same area.

In 2010, I was invited again to India, this time to conduct disability training, in collaboration with local pastors, church leaders, medical professionals, social workers, community workers, and disability groups. The training was conducted in eight different cities over a 7-1/2 week period with between 40 to 120 people attending each of these training events. The focus of this disability training was to encourage the people of India to integrate people with disabilities into their community and church.

John, learning to use a transfer board

The following report provides a detailed narrative account of the training sessions, with the reactions of those who took part, including persons with disabilities, their families, and the disability community. Additionally, I was able to share my personal experiences as a person with a disability in India today as compared to what it was like 35 years ago when I lived there. As a result of my travels and observation, I was able to offer some future recommendations for disability advocates in India to consider as they continue to advance the cause of people with disabilities.

Preparation

As with my previous trips to India, it was critical that I assemble a qualified team of volunteers to accompany me to India. This included choosing team members who had some experience and /or an interest in working with the disability community, as well as a willingness to learn from both our team from the United States and the local team. Also of importance was that each team member had to be willing to pay their own way or raise the funds for the trip. The team of 2010 was a unique team, being composed of two teams who were going to India for a similar purpose, and agreeing to join and work together in some cities in India.

Team one included **Karen**, a trained physical therapist, who had accompanied me on two previous trips to India in 2006 and 2008. Karen has been my support in the USA as well as on other trips. She assisted me with material preparation for the conferences, has taught alongside me, and has been a personal assistant to me on these trips. **Amanda** was a student at Moody Bible Institute (MBI) in Chicago, majoring in Pre-counseling. She developed an interest in India and the disability community while working for me as my personal assistant. **Hannah** was also a student at MBI with a major in Women's ministry. Hannah had developed an interest in India after hearing a pastor from India speak, and from Amanda who spoke of her personal interest in India. Amanda and Hannah both wanted to learn as much they could about how to serve the disability community in India and about its culture, so they committed to join us on this trip during their spring break.

Team two included **Jon** and **Vicky** who travel to India two to three times a year to provide support to people with quadriplegia. They also participate in workshops sponsored by various organizations that educate people about the importance of independence for people with quadriplegia. Jon was twenty-three years old, and at the time, a student. When he was nineteen, he fell approximately 70 ft from a mountain in India. As a result, he became a quadriplegic. Since his life in a wheelchair started in India, he has developed a special compassion for the people with quadriplegia in India and a desire to help them. Vicky is Jon's mother, who assists with his work and was his travel partner during this trip. She is gifted in networking, and is a motivational speaker. **George** is Jon's friend and his care giver. George's desire was to learn the culture of India. He was a great help and support, not only to Jon, but to all of us. More will be said about their specific assignments later in the report.

Collaborating partner organizations were identified after months of communication through emails, phone calls, and Skype conference calls by both teams nationally and internationally. It was a tedious process to determine the organizations with which we could work well together. Both teams had different commitments, which meant that they would not be able to work together in some of the cities visited. The following report focuses entirely on the cities that I personally visited.

The trip took eight months of planning, including assembling my team of professionals and students with skills who would benefit the goal of the trip and communicate with the groups in India concerning the conference details. Karen and I prepared the material for the seminars, workshops and other teachings for each city. Two months prior to departure, we finalized dates and purchased both international flights to India and domestic flights within India. Wheelchair accessible accommodations had to be found for me, and reservations needed to be made. Many of my contacts in India offered their homes for us to stay, but usually Indian homes are very difficult for people in wheelchairs to maneuver.

Though it is difficult for people with disabilities to travel within the USA, it is much more difficult overseas. As a wheelchair user, I had to be aware of the need, not only for my protection, but also the protection of my wheelchair. Without my wheelchair, I would be significantly more disabled. One bathroom on the plane is accessible, but it is not the most convenient for a person with physical limitations. A passenger who cannot walk or stand can be transported to the bathroom but not easily or quickly, and he/she will still need assistance in the bathroom. Sitting for many hours is always a challenge, as well.

Normally, I use a power-assisted wheelchair or scooter for travel in my home city of Chicago, and I am very independent as a wheelchair user. The most difficult part of traveling to India begins the moment I leave my front door. Someone is needed to push my manual wheelchair, as I do not have the

Aircraft aisle chair

arm strength to push my wheels forward over long distances. Even though many international airplanes, such as Boeing 747, are considered accessible, I must rely on my travel companions to assist me in the bathroom. Typically, I have to wait between 10-60 minutes for the flight attendant to bring the aisle chair to transport me to the bathroom. Next, my travel companions check the chair to confirm that I am securely positioned. Crew members then push me up to the bathroom door, and some are willing to push me in. My travel companions then assist me in the bathroom. The whole process can take a minimum of 45 minutes, if the crew responds to my call quickly, which rarely happens.

Airline and airport staffs in India are even less trained and equipped to help people with disabilities. The major fear I have while traveling is that my wheelchair will be put in the baggage compartment and not be available upon disembarking the plane. Were this to happen, the aisle chair, which is very unstable, would be used to push me, presenting a dangerous situation for me. These chairs are not made to transport people across the building. Another fear is that my chair will be damaged in the cargo hold and not be able to be repaired at the airport, which would make it very difficult for me and my travel companions.

Though traveling does provoke anxiety, there is also a great amount of excitement. I look forward with great anticipation to connecting and reconnecting with people in India. In 2010, upon arriving in New Delhi, Karen and I stayed with some of my relatives. There we rested for a couple of days to recover from jet lag, and then visited friends and ministry contacts.

After visiting and resting, we began doing some networking in New Delhi for a conference that was scheduled a month after our arrival. Following the networking and finalizing the details for the conference, which was a month later, we departed for the city of Varanasi.

Varanasi was my home for 20 years, where I grew up and completed Junior College (equivalent to high school in US). It is there that I had built the most significant relationships. As a child, I thought I was one of the few people with a disability in Varanasi, until I visited the homes of some of my friends. While visiting their families, I discovered there were many children and adults with disabilities who were shut-ins.

Karen and I were looking forward to traveling there to start collaborating with the church. I was so looking forward to seeing my friends in Varanasi, and Karen was looking forward to meeting them and getting to know them.

2
Varanasi

Varanasi, also known as Banaras or Kashi, is one of the oldest, continuously populated cities in the world, and the oldest city in India. Located on the west bank of the Ganges River (considered sacred by Hindus), Varanasi welcomes more than one million Hindu pilgrims each year, who bathe in the sacred river and visit the shrine to Kashi Vishwanath (a manifestation of the Hindu god "Shiva"). In addition to the Hindu pilgrims, many international tourists pass through Varanasi on their way to Sarnath, six miles from Varanasi and one of the four sacred cities in Buddhism and where Gautam Buddha delivered his first message to his disciples. It contains the most extensive ruins among places on the Buddhist trail, some of which date back to the third century BCE (Before Common Era).

Ganges river at Varanasi

Nearly five million people, predominantly Hindu, call Varanasi home. The city boasts of a wealth of activities and organizations committed to fine

15

arts, local crafts and education. These handicrafts include creation of glass bangles and bracelets, fashioning brass collectibles, ornamental furniture, and embroidery of silk saris with gold and silver thread. Saris are the traditional clothing of Indian women, comprised of six-yards of fabric, which is draped around the waist and shoulder in an elegant manner. Four universities are located in Varanasi, as well as many colleges, schools and hospitals. The primary industry in Varanasi is manufacturing, although nearly three-fourths of the population is unemployed.

Among the groups most affected by unemployment is the disability community. Few organizations exist that provide rehabilitation and training services to persons with disabilities, and those organizations that do are sometimes threatened by various socio-political or religious groups. Unfortunately, this has made it difficult in the past to encourage more people to become involved in helping those with disabilities. Because of this history and the time constraints, it would be difficult for us to do much more than lay the groundwork for future presentations on disability awareness. However, as it happened, we had many opportunities to share our stories, to teach people in Varanasi about disabilities, and to encourage them to help people with disabilities in whatever way possible.

Upon our arrival in Varanasi, Pastor James and his wife, Laura, met us at the hotel. I had known Pastor James since we were children, due to the fact that our fathers, who were both pastors, had occasionally worked together. Before his parents retired, they were my host family in Varanasi during my earlier trips. Then when his dad retired, Pastor James and Laura hosted my later trips.

At the hotel, we discussed the schedule for the week. On the first day, there would be a women's retreat, and on second and third day, a pastor's retreat and a prayer day for pastors, respectively. We stayed at the hotel for a couple of days, giving us the opportunity to organize our activities for the week. The hotel was our temporary quarters until we could move into the church guestroom where an attached, accessible bathroom was being built, according to my design and measurement recommendations, as requested during the previous year's visit. This request was due, in part, because during the previous year, my travel companion had to push my wheelchair a few blocks back to our hotel so I could use the hotel's accessible facilities. Since the church was already planning to remodel, they had asked for my suggestions. In addition to the bathroom, I also recommended they add a kitchenette, since there was still adequate space remaining to allow self-sufficiency for guests who are elderly or who have disabilities. From what I had previously learned in my classes at the University of Illinois at Chicago, I shared with them information about standard measurements for accessible plumbing fixtures (toilet, sink, shower), all of which they greatly appreciated.

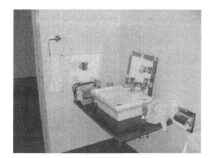 

Accessible bathroom in Varanasi

By the time Karen and I arrived in 2010, most of the work on the bathroom had been completed. We were asked to look at the room to help them decide where every decorative fixture (grab bars, towel rack, soap & toothbrush holder, etc.) should be installed. Since I did not have the standard measurements with me in India, I wheeled around the room, pointing out positions for the fixtures that would also accommodate a person with a lower wheelchair than mine was. Two days later, everything was completed, except for the vessel sink and the counter. The vessel sink sits above the counter like a bowl, and due to the height of the counter, was not accessible to wheelchair users. Therefore, the counter was lowered five to six inches to accommodate a wheelchair. Unfortunately, that meant a person using a wheelchair would not be able to fit his/her knees under the counter to use the sink comfortably. So, I recommended that the counter be rounded inward, which allows the wheelchair to move closer to the sink. After two days to complete that change and a few other minor improvements, everything was finished and worked perfectly.

My Childhood Neighborhood Revisited

On our first day, Karen and I had the afternoon and evening open, so we decided to visit my old neighborhood in Varanasi where many of my friends still live. When I was growing up in Varanasi, my family lived in a predominantly Muslim community. For a long time, we were the only Christians in the area. During that time in that area, Muslims felt much more comfortable and in unity with Christians, due to the commonality of the monotheistic belief of the two faiths. Consequently, our families socialized together, ate together, and helped each other in various ways with true concern for one another. Hospitals and doctors referred to my mother as a "social worker," because she was always accompanying people to the hospital or guiding doctors to home visits for medical purposes. Our neighbors were very dear to us. I lived in that neighborhood longer than all my five siblings, so I became very close with many of my neighbors. Even after moving to the United States and being away from India for 35 year, I still kept in touch with most of them.

One of the primary reasons I wanted to visit my old neighborhood was to visit a family I had been close to and who had just lost their mother, Zara. When I look back, I believe this was the family where my disability ministry/ service began. The first child in this family, Shannan*, was a beautiful girl but spoiled, given inordinate attention from the whole family. Their second child, Shabeena,* was just as beautiful as her sister, but she developed severe scoliosis at the age of three or four months. As she grew, she developed a hunchback, which stunted her growth. Because she was not a demanding child, Shabeena received very little attention from her family.

My mother and I felt saddened that Shabeena was neglected by her family, so I asked her mother, Zara, if I could care for Shabeena part of the day in my home. She was thrilled, so every morning Zara would bathe, change and feed Shabeena, and then bring her to my home between 10 and 11 in the morning, with an extra bottle and change of clothes. Shabeena would stay with me during the day; and every few hours, Zara would check to see if the baby needed more milk or a clean diaper. Other than those brief visits, Shabeena was with me almost eight hours a day. She became very attached to me. My mom and our hired cook would also help care for Shabeena, while I focused on my studies. I was only in the 7th grade and home-schooled at the time, so consequently, my schedule was flexible. I was being home-schooled because the neighborhood schools did not accept children with disabilities, primarily because of the inaccessibility. In the evening, I had a tutor come to help me with certain subjects, so Shabeena would go home to her family.

As I had helped Zara with Shabeena, there were situations in which Zara helped me. Growing up with disabilities presents many barriers. Children and young people with disabilities need encouragement to believe in the abilities they do have. The following is a story from my personal life. It reveals how my mother's fear, because of her love, became a barrier to some areas of my development. However, Zara's trust in my ability allowed me to build my confidence, beginning my journey toward independence.

Zara was my first cooking teacher. My mother feared that I would injure myself, so she never allowed me near the stove. However, I was desperate to learn the craft of cooking. My opportunity came one morning at Zara's home. I had just arrived as she was about to instruct her daughters about the day's cooking assignments. Shannon, Shabeena's older sister, was eight years old and had the task of preparing lunch. Zara asked me if I wanted to cook, not knowing of my mother's instruction to stay away from the stove. I quickly responded that "I would love to help, but sadly, my mother has forbidden me to do something she considered so dangerous for me." Zara emphatically replied, "You can do it!" Her optimistic statement encouraged me, and I responded with a resounding "Yes! as long as my mother doesn't see me." Zara instructed her two older girls to help me and sent Shera to be on the "lookout," in case my mother decided to "surprise" us with a visit.

I started my first cooking experience, sitting on a very low stool in front of the stove. The stove was fifteen inches off the ground, constructed out of brick and clay. There were two burners for the fire, one with coal and the other with wood logs. The girls helped me put a big pot on the stove, and slowly I began to follow the recipe that Zara had verbally given to me. About forty-five minutes later, the youngest daughter called out, "Mama is coming! Mama is coming!" Zara immediately ran over to my side in the kitchen, she picked me up, and moved me to the opposite side of the room. Then she calmly sat next to the stove and finished stirring the pot that was almost finished cooking. My mama never suspected that I had been cooking. Later, as we began eating, Mama returned, inquiring if I was ready for lunch. Zara invited her to join us for lunch, and before Mama had an opportunity to say "yes" or "no," Zara immediately served her a plate of food. While eating, Mama began to express approval of the food and especially the cook, asking who had done the preparation. To her surprise, Zara informed her, "today, Joy has cooked," explaining how the girls had helped while Zara kept a close eye on the project.

Needless to say, from that point on, Mama gave me more freedom in the kitchen, allowing me near the stove. Whenever the girls in the neighborhood had their daily cooking assignment, I was allowed to join them. It was here that my first cooking lessons started.

Zara's trust in my ability also opened her eyes to see the abilities that her own Shabeena had. Throughout her growing-up years, Zara continued to encourage Shabeena, which was needed to develop and maximize her skills..

Today, Shabeena is an intelligent, hardworking woman, and holds three different jobs. She completed her Master's degree and also completed training in gold and silver threaded embroidery design used in creating silk saris. Shabeena's primary job is teaching at a local secondary school (equivalent to junior high and high school in the United States). She also directs a home-based afterschool program that was started by her mother. Children from the neighborhood come to be tutored and receive help with homework. Shabeena receives a monthly fee for each child in the program. Utilizing her talent and love for art, her third job is drawing patterns to be embroidered on saris. Shabeena and her sister Shannan share their income to take care of the expenses at home.

Shannan had kept in close touch with me over the years and kept me informed of the welfare of the family. As Karen and I headed to visit them, I mentioned to Karen that this would be a very different visit because the family would be seeing me for the first time since their mother's passing, and there would be some crying.

Many homes in Varanasi are similar to row houses in the United States with several homes connected together. Others are designed more like condominiums or townhomes. Varanasi is comprised of neighborhoods approximately one square mile in diameter. Shabeena's home is situated about 40 feet from the main street in one of these residential areas. Homes in this area are behind several stores as well as a large mosque, which has been part of the community for nearly a century. Running between the mosque on the right and the homes on the left is a narrow walkway, approximately six to ten feet wide. Since it was not wide enough for a vehicle, I was pushed in my wheelchair down the cracked, uneven concrete walkway in my wheelchair, which is not an easy or comfortable ride. On the right, was a storm drain full of dirty water and a neighborhood dump site where residents dump their trash until the city sanitation department picks it up every other week. The stench was quite bad, and I had to be careful not to allow my wheelchair to go through the trash or the filthy water.

Shabeena's home is directly at the end of the walkway. As we knocked on the door, Shannan opened it. Entering into Shabeena's home was a bit difficult for me. Two young men had to carry my wheelchair over the first threshold, which was about two to three inches high. Thresholds are an important part of Indian architecture. They define the home's space and keep out crawling insects and snakes. A few feet inside the first threshold there is an even higher threshold, about six to eight inches high. The same two young men also carried my wheelchair over the second threshold into the courtyard. I was reminded that prior to receiving my first wheelchair, I had to crawl to get around. Due to having to travel that way, I did not like these thresholds. With the use of a wheelchair, I dislike them even more. They are a huge hindrance, but this is a typical feature in most Indian households, especially in the older homes.

Shortly thereafter, the family came out to greet me. According to the Muslim culture, male and females do not hug or shake hands with a person of the opposite sex, unless she is their mother, sister, or daughter. However, as soon as I entered the house, Shabeena's father gave me a hug, treating me like a sister, crying uncontrollably and saying about his late wife, "She is gone! Your sister is gone." After a minute, or so, he moved away, trying to control his sobbing. I remained to console his children and grandchildren, as they came forward hugging, crying, grieving.

The courtyard of the house was spacious enough to set up six to eight single beds during summertime. To the left of the courtyard, was a tiny bedroom for Shabeena's father. Beyond that, was the kitchen, tucked out of sight of the guests. On the far right were two small rooms, each with a single step as you entered. The first room contains a spigot for hand washing and a bucket for bathing. To bathe, a person sits on a stool, and fills a tumbler with water from the bucket and pours it on himself/herself. If desired, the water can be heated on the stove in the kitchen and mixed with the cooler water in the bucket. The second room has a pour-flush squat toilet, not convenient for wheelchair users as the door is very narrow and inside there is only enough room for one person. The major reason for keeping the showers and the toilets separate is for convenience, so that both could be used at the same time by two different people. In more modern homes in India, the sink, toilet and shower are in the same room (in wealthier homes, a tub as well), along with modern plumbing and an electric shower head heater, called a geyser.

Beyond the courtyard is a long veranda with a couple of wooden beds and some chairs where Shabeena's students study. Past the veranda is a large room that serves as a sleeping area during cooler months. In the far left of the room, there were a couple of double beds that are likely shared by family members. In the middle of the room, there is a king sized jute mat covered with bed sheets. A couple of folded quilts and several pillows are positioned against the wall, used to make beds at night. During the daytime, the same jute mat is used to sit on for meals, tea, and entertaining guests. On the right side of the room, there are a few chairs and a small coffee table. To the far right, there is a small room with a door that was remained closed during my entire visit. I recall that room being used as a bedroom by Shabeena's parents when they first married, but I believe it is now used for storing the family's clothes or personal belongings.

Karen and Shabeena sat in the chairs on the right side of the room, as I wheeled myself over to sit by them. Shabeena's father sat on the floor against the pillows with a quilt protecting him against the chill. It was wintertime, and the house was cold, since Indian homes do not have heating. As we were gathered together, I remembered spending time with the family in this same spot, playing board games, or having tea and snacks. As we continued to visit, the sun began to set, and they turned on a dim light. In spite of limited resources, this dear family showed us warm hospitality and love.

In time, the two sisters shared how their mother passed away. Not wanting to ask too many questions and remind them of their pain, I just listened and interpreted for Karen. They were speaking in the Urdu language, which comes from Arabic and which most Muslims in India and Pakistan speak. Karen and I spent most of the evening with them, even as other neighbors came to see us. My visit brought back so many wonderful memories of the years I lived next door to this family.

The home I grew up in was comprised of three levels (the first level contained rooms, verandas, kitchen area, bathroom and toilet, the second contained rooms and verandas, and the third level was a terrace). Our house shared a wall with Shabeena's house. Even though my bedroom was on the first floor, there were three very high steps leading into my room, which were difficult to negotiate. Nonetheless, I did it several times a day. I remember some rare occasions when I ventured up to the second floor. Crawling up a flight of narrow steps was especially unpleasant, because there was a wall on the left side of the staircase and a railing with no wall on the right side. I feared many times of falling through the railing. After we reminisced about other shared memories, Karen and I said our "goodbyes" and returned to our hotel room.

Women's Retreat

The next morning, Karen and I met with Pastor James to continue preparing for the conference. Though the focus of my work is to serve people with disabilities and to train others to do the same, I agreed to preach from the Bible, as Pastor James suggested I do during my time there. However, I prayed that the overall focus of the conference would change, with the emphasis on disability awareness and teaching people how to serve people with disabilities and motivating others to serve.

Two days after Karen and I arrived, Jon, Vicky and George joined us. The guestroom was completed, so Karen and I were able to move out of the hotel, allowing Jon to use what was the only accessible room in the hotel. That night our entire team met with Pastor James and his wife, Laura, to discuss the details of the conference program. Pastor James asked, "On what topics would you like to speak?" Since we were speaking to a church group, it was important to approach our topics with a Biblical point of view. Jon said he would speak on suffering, especially the need to remember God in the midst of suffering, as the story of Job in the Bible illustrates. Vicky would share how a disability impacts a family from a parent's point of view. In our earlier conversation with Pastor James, we had talked about learning disabilities, so he suggested Karen talk about learning disabilities. I planned to talk about God's heart for persons with disabilities and our responsibility toward them. Following our opening presentations, the focus of the conference began to turn more toward that of disability awareness, as I had prayed and desired it would.

The first day of our presentations began with a Women's Retreat. Retreats are organized by churches to provide spiritual rejuvenation, emotional renewal, and in some instances, physical rest for attendees. In India, retreats are often held for only one day, so as to not impose a financial hardship or family burden on those attending. I had been at the Women's Retreat in 2009 at the same church, where I spoke at four or five different sessions throughout the day. At the end of that retreat, women were challenged to become more involved in their church, not only for their own benefit but also for the sake of others. After the Retreat, anecdotes related to my experience as a person with disabilities suggested that my challenges were effective in that many could relate to them at some level.

There was a young woman at that 2009 retreat who walked with a limp, due to polio. She had said to the pastor's wife at one point: "You don't understand. Because of my disability I can't do many things. And I do not want to travel to church, because when I walk, people look at me strangely." At the end of the day, this same young woman came forward and confessed to the other women who had attended that she had been making excuses, saying, "If Joy can travel across the world in her wheelchair to encourage people, then I can walk with a limp to go to church and help other young people." Later, I was informed that the young lady had been very active in her church community during the previous year and had come again for the 2010 retreat.

Another woman, who had attended the 2009 retreat, admitted that she never thought she could do anything to help a family in her neighborhood who had a child with a disability. By the end of the retreat, she was planning on telling the mother of that child she would be willing to spend one Sunday morning a month with her child with a disability, so that this mother could attend church. By the end of the 2009 retreat, 40 of the 65 women attendees had decided to work alongside the church to help with the church's activities in general, to the amazement of the pastor's wife. While the women at the 2009 retreat were all from the same church, an invitation was extended to women from other churches around the city for the 2010 retreat, totaling 125 attendees. Since many women had not attended the 2009 retreat, I repeated my life story and worked it into the teaching that was planned. The title was, "Responsibility of the Church for the Disabled." During my presentation, I focused on the Biblical directive for churches to accept responsibility for people with disabilities in their communities, as mandated in a passage of scripture in the Bible. The discussion challenged those in attendance that all have an obligation to follow the Biblical charge to "bring the poor, maimed, lame, and blind" into the "house of God" (Luke 14:23), thus embracing them and assisting them in their need. Also, in learning the "Four Eternal Truths," the attendees were exhorted to follow the example of Abraham, urging the audience to remain obedient to God in all situations and allowing Him to honor their obedience.

After lunch, I spoke about "But He is Strong" in the additional session. The subject's intent was to remind people that God has a plan and purpose for their lives. Even if God does not heal someone from disability or terminal illness, He will bring other forms of healing into his or her life. We are made "perfect in weakness," because He is our strength. (Holy Bible: The New Testament, 2 Corinthians 12:9, 10 NKJV)

Throughout the day, as I talked about disability issues and opened the floor to questions and comments, I discovered many women who either had a disability of their own or had a family member or acquaintance with a disability. Several members of other churches realized for the first time how hard it is for mothers of a child with disability. They made a commitment to help those mothers, both as individuals and as a group. One of the women, a teacher, offered to tutor a child with a disability who was not attending school. Another decided that, since she did not even know how many families in her church and community had family members with disabilities, she would make a conscious effort to find out who they were to offer support.

I explained to the women that it is much easier to work toward a common cause and encouraged them to share with their congregations what they had learned at the retreat. The women considered these small beginnings as an opportunity to improve the disability community, and were eager to do more. During my next visit, I hoped to share in several sessions ways to help the disability community.

At the end of the day, as people were coming to meet me and to ask questions, a little girl named Rajni, a polio survivor, was carried by her sister to the front where I was sitting. Rajni crawled closer in order to talk with me. As we talked, I asked her what grade she was in school. She told me that schools in her community would not accept her because of her disability. Later, I talked to the pastor and asked him to find out more about Rajni's situation: "Who rejected her application and what were the reasons for denying her admission." I encouraged him to try to share with, and hopefully convince, the school that education is just as important for children with disabilities as for those without and to explain to the parents that, if Rajni is admitted, they needed to commit to getting her to school every day.

Meeting with Church Leadership

The next day a meeting for pastors, their wives, and other church leaders was conducted. Jon shared the Biblical story about Job, a man who stayed faithful to God in spite of the loss of his family, property, and health.

Using this text as his example, Jon shared further about the need to stay faithful to God through our suffering, and how God gives us the courage and strength to face hard times. Additionally, Jon reminded us how God has blessed us in various other ways, including using our suffering to encourage others.

In the next session, Vicky, Jon's mother, shared about her family's experience of having to face the sudden disability of their son, due to an accident. Vicky's synopsis of Jon's journey disclosed that in 2006 Jon fell off a cliff in India, broke his neck, but survived. So began a long and painful walk of faith. As the result of this family's walk, Jon has gained an ardent love for the people of India and a kinship with the people around the world who have suffered long term debilitating injuries. Both Jon and Vicky conclude that while there is suffering in the world, God's redemptive love and transforming power can turn a horrible event into a personal triumph.

Next day on Sunday afternoon at the Pastor's prayer time we were not scheduled to provide any teaching or presentation. However, Pastor James asked if one of us would be willing to share a short message before the prayer time. For the first 20 minutes, Vicky spoke on suffering. By the end of the day, though we were pleased with what had been accomplished, we were physically exhausted. To relax, we, as a team, walked to a shopping mall nearby to enjoy some ice cream. Returning to our rooms, we packed in preparation for our next morning departure for Kachhwa.

3

Kachhwa

Leaving Varanasi, we traveled about 20 miles (30 km) south to the city of Kachhwa, located in the southwest corner in the state of Uttar Pradesh (North State). Kachhwa has a population of 14,712, 54 percent male and 46 percent female. Since 2001, the literacy rate has remained at approximately 57 percent, which is lower than the 59.5 percent national average.

In Kachhwa, we met with Dr. Raju Abraham, the director of Kachhwa Christian Hospital (KCH). This hospital has a long history. It was founded over 100 years ago by Dr. Neville Everad, a medical missionary with the Bible Churchmen's Missionary Society (BCMS). At that time, the hospital had only 15 beds. In the 1960's, my parents traveled to Kachhwa twice a month to minister to the spiritual needs of the hospital's large Christian staff. The nearby villages had no churches, so my parents provided spiritual support to the people in the surrounding communities, as well. As a child I had often heard about the hospital from my parents but had never visited the facility. My parents travelled by bus between Varanasi and Kachhwa, and since I did not have a wheelchair at that time, it required that they physically carry me wherever we went.

I had heard many stories from my parents about the kindness, hospitality, and desire for spiritual support from among the people in Kachhwa   At the hospital, there were persons on staff who had children my age, and my mother planned special sessions soley for the children. I had hoped that if it was possible for me to go, that I would be able to meet all the wonderful people and the children my parents frequently talked about.

In the early 1970's, the quality of care of the hospital began to decline, as its financial support decreased, resulting in difficulty maintaining adequate staffing levels. In 2002, with the hospital on the brink of foreclosure, new staff and improved outreach programs to 90 villages enabled it to make a comeback. In 2010, I finally had an opportunity to visit this wonderful hospital which I had heard so much about as a child.

I had heard about Dr. Raju but had never met him. He started working at the time the hospital was in danger of closing. Since Kachhwa Christian Hospital is the only hospital in the community and serving several nearby villages, its closing would have deprived the community of essential medical care. The closest hospitals to Kachhwa and the surrounding villages were in Varanasi, a two hour drive by car, and most people in the villages in Kachhwa could not afford cars nor had the money to rent a taxi. Since Dr. Raju and his wife assumed the leadership of the hospital, it has grown from 15 to 20 in-patient beds and serves 30,000 patients a year. Dental and ophthalmology departments have also been added. The ophthalmology department conducts approximately 3000 eye surgeries per year, mostly removing cataracts.

Settling In

Dr. Raju had sent a driver and vehicle to Varanasi to transport us to the hospital. Our team, along with two wheelchairs and luggage, piled into the vehicle, and thankfully everything fit. I sat in the front passenger seat as the front door has a wider opening, making it easier for me to transfer with a transfer board and to use the seatbelt. In India, the law is stricter about the use of seatbelts for the driver and the front passenger. Jon was in the backseat with George, who served as his personal seatbelt. The others crowded into the backseat with George and Jon, and they resembled a can of sardines! As we approached the hospital, we saw a large gate with the sign, reading "Kachhwa Christian Hospital." We were welcomed by Dr. Raju's wife and a few staff members, who escorted us to the guesthouse, which contained two bedrooms, each with three beds. The women occupied the bedroom that had an attached bathroom, and the men slept in the bedroom with a bathroom adjacent to their room.

We were excited to discover that a new ramp had been installed, in preparation for our arrival. However, soon after settling into the guesthouse, our team noticed that the bathroom doors were very narrow. For me to use the bathroom, Karen had to force my wheelchair through the narrow door, while carefully lowering my wheelchair down a small step below the doorway. The bathroom was sub-divided into two sections: the first section contained the sink and mirror, and the second section a partially enclosed shower, a toilet without grab bars and a very small turn-around room for my wheelchair. Knowing this would make it difficult for both Jon and me to use the facilities independently. I was comforted by the fact that we had a capable support team to assist us.

Once settled in our room, we freshened up and left the guesthouse, touring another building on the hospital campus that had a new ramp. This building contained the living quarters for Dr. Raju and his wife, as well as the administrative offices. Dr. Raju joined us for tea in the staff dining room, introducing us to several staff members. We had been invited to the hospital to provide disability training to the staff and to determine how the hospital could serve the disability community. Over a cup of tea, we shared the details of the training with Dr. Raju, outlining what each team member would be doing over the next three days. Jon and I would share our personal stories of living with quadriplegia and paraplegia with the staff in smaller groups at different times throughout our stay at the hospital. Jon had a personal DVD documentary for this purpose. We had also prepared training material on various aspects of disability, including functional, cognitive, and social issues.

Then we would spend the second half of our second day with two groups of primary leadership staff, at which time they would view Jon's documentary. After sharing our stories and experiences, Jon and I would then talk about various aspects of disabilities and how they impact individuals and their families.

Training Day

At 7:30 the next morning, our second day began. I was invited to speak during the hospital's morning devotions and prayer time. Karen helped me dress and pushed my wheelchair to the building next door for the devotion service. About 50 people from the nearby villages were there. The majority were Christians, some related to hospital staff and others from different faith groups.

During this time, I shared my story using Bible passages and simple language to express my thoughts. I knew that 90 percent of my listeners had very limited education and spoke a dialect in which I was no longer fluent. I also spoke about our responsibility toward people with disabilities and used the parable of the Great Banquet as an illustration. In this passage (Luke 14:21), the writer concludes that God's house is to be filled with people both with and without disabilities. The application is that we are all God's creation, and therefore, we all have intrinsic value. Consequently, it is each person's obligation to respond to all people with love, respect, and kindness.

After this presentation, the villagers had several questions, but due to time constraints, I was only able to answer a few. One villager asked, "Do we know why innocent children end up with disability?" I discussed the role of infection, malnutrition, and lack of medical care for mothers during pregnancy, with special emphasis on increased risk for those with disability. Other villagers contributed their understanding, by giving examples from their family or their village.

Another participant asked, "How do we help individuals with disabilities and their families?" I explained how all mothers have enormous responsibilities, including cooking, cleaning, and providing care for their children. Providing care for a child with disability takes an even greater amount of time and effort, and therefore, creates more work for the mother. It would be helpful for those in the community, who do not have a child with a disability or younger children to care for, to volunteer to watch the child, giving the mother a much needed respite from her daily responsibilities. This also would give the child the opportunity to socialize with others in the community. I emphasized how important this was, given the stigma attached to disabilities.

What I wanted them to take away from our time together was that we are all God's creation, so we should help each other, care for those who cannot care for themselves, and treat everyone equally, with respect. I also encouraged them not to treat a child or adult with a disability like an outcast from society, but as their neighbor and friend.

Polio Survivors Serving Others with Disabilities

After breakfast, Dr. Raju and I met with three young men, William, Mark, and Henry, who were members of a post-polio group from the various villages the hospital serves. Polio affected each of these three men differently. William walks with a severe limp. Mark has a weak right leg and walks with a slight limp. Henry is unable to walk. Henry rides a hand driven tricycle,

Mark, Henry and William

similar to rickshaw. And where his tricycle cannot go, his friends and family will carry him. All three have completed their Bachelor's degrees. These young men, along with seven other post-polio men and women, started their own non-government organization (NGO) to educate people with disabilities and their families in nearby villages about available government benefits.

When Dr. Raju and I met with William, Mark, and Henry, they had already been in contact with several families affected by disabilities. Since they, like I, were post-polio, Dr. Raju thought it would be encouraging for them to meet me, so that I could share with them ideas and suggestions that might help them serve the disability community better. As we talked, the young men shared photographs and the data on each individual with disabilities they had interviewed, explaining that they had questioned them about their disability, age, educational background, and work history, and what government benefits they were receiving, what benefits they needed, and what help would be beneficial to them. Some of those interviewed were already receiving disability benefits, while others had no idea what was available to them. So the young men were going door-to-door to educate people about available services for people with disabilities. An example of a service is a free bus pass, which is similar to a free bus pass through the Circuit Breaker program in the state of Illinois. Even people who were completely bedridden were told about the bus pass, so they could share the information with others who might benefit from the program. Brochures are printed about these and other government programs, as well as being advertised in the newspapers. However, since many families do not receive a newspaper, these young men distribute the brochures to those who can read and explain the information to those who are unable to read. They also accompany clients to government offices and assist them in applying for benefits.

Dr. Raju and I were very impressed that the young men had compiled so much information and organized it so well. Since they knew more than I did about the various disability benefit programs in India and were educating the local people about them, I simply encouraged them to continue the work they were doing. Then, I briefly shared some of my experiences as an individual with post-polio growing up in India at a time when none of these benefits were available to me. No one was providing this type of support to the disability community at that time, which this NGO was now providing.

Later, Dr. Raju and I discussed different possibilities as to how the hospital could help this NGO in its effort to better serve people with disabilities. I expressed that by partnering with them the NGO would gain credibility, making it easier for them to acquire the trust of the people in the community. The hospital staff could direct patients with disabilities to the NGO to learn about benefits available to them. In turn, the NGO could educate their clientele about the importance of getting regular medical care and direct them to the hospital. As we continued talking, Dr. Raju considered partnering with the NGO. Details of the partnership and determining what things they could collaborate on would be decided later.

Dr. Raju and our team talked about what KCH could do to help the disability community. We suggested that since the needs of the disability community are so vast, that the hospital could not possibly address everything, so the decision was made to choose a couple of needs that would have an immediate impact on the community. The consensus was that accessible toilets would be the hospital's first focus.

In India most of the homes and huts in the villages have just one or two rooms where the families live. During the warmer weather, villagers sleep outdoors on cots in front of their small homes. However, during the winter, there is not enough room for all of the family members to have cots inside the house, so they sleep on the dirt floor. Jute mats would be placed on the floor, and homemade quilts were used as mattresses and blankets. Similarly, during the warmer weather, cooking is done outside on a stove made out of clay and bricks. The same kind of stove is built inside the house to be used during severe winter

Joy meets Dr. Raju

or heavy rains. The stoves use wood, coal, or cow dung patties from the small farms nearby. Those families who own a cow for milk and a bull (for plowing) do not have to search for or buy cow dung to make the patties.

Some villages have what are referred to as public bathrooms or toilets, often a half mile from their housing, while others have no public toilets, and so the people relieve themselves in the nearby fields. Many villagers actually prefer to go in the field, because the public toilets are very dirty. No one wants the responsibility for cleaning the community toilets, due to the fact that the cleaning of the toilets is done by the Dalits (the lowest cast), who are hired for the job. The risk in using the fields is that snakes and other pests inhabit the farm fields. Naturally, the risks are greater for those who cannot stand or run.

I was familiar with the toilet situation in the villages, and I explained to Dr. Raju that for people with disabilities to reach a toilet, they often must crawl over hot concrete in summer and through mud during the rainy season. After learning this, Dr. Raju decided the priority project would be building toilets, either inside or nearby outside their homes, for families who have family members with disabilities. He had already started a toilet project for the villagers, though not specifically with needs of the people with disabilities in mind. The project required determining what accessibility features would be needed. This led to an in-depth discussion about adaptations that would be required and workable to accommodate a variety of different individuals with different needs. For example, an individual who is able to stand but unable to bend his/her knees to sit in a squat position would need a western-style toilet with a higher accessibility height and grab bars on both sides for support. An individual who is unable to stand and is forced to crawl because they do not have a wheelchair would need a toilet bowl not too high off the ground. In these instances, the lower part of the toilet bowl would need to be put underground, so people who crawl can reach the toilet seat easily. Sometimes the water tank for the toilets in the villages is high and has a flush chain that can only be reached by those who can stand. For someone who cannot stand, though, the chain must be extended. Additional adaptations must be made when there is no running water and buckets of water are used for manual flushing. In these instances, the person with a disability would need the help of a friend or family member.

Dr. Raju redirected some of the funding set aside to build toilets for the general community to include building accessible facilities as well. Working together, Dr. Raju, his staff, and our team selected those families for the first six accessible toilets. The local team would go to the homes to evaluate the people who were to receive a toilet, decide where the toilet would be placed, and determine what adaptations would be needed. The first recipient was a man named Thomas, who had difficulty walking, due to arthritis. He was able to bend one knee with great difficulty, and the other knee did not bend at all. At the hospital, Thomas had been receiving treatment for various medical conditions, but until now, the hospital staff had not realized his difficulty in using the Indian style toilet. Another recipient was Henry, one of the three post-polio men (from the NGO which educates people about available governmental disability benefits). Henry needed an accessible toilet, since he was unable to walk. The third recipient was a 12 year old girl named Dolly. Dolly had a brittle bone disease, which had stunted her growth, resulting in her looking like a six year old. A fourth accessible toilet would be installed at the hospital for use by clinic patients, and the remaining two toilets would be installed in the hospital guest rooms where we were staying. Until Jon and I arrived, Dr. Raju and his staff had not realized how inaccessible the hospital's guesthouse bathrooms were for people in wheelchairs. In preparing for our visit, the hospital had installed ramps at three different locations for our convenience in navigating the hospital campus, but it never occurred to them to consider the accessibility of the toilets and bathrooms. It was encouraging to see how our presence at the hospital could positively influence such an investment of time and resources in improving the lives of people with disabilities in the community. Lastly, I demonstrated to the medical staff simple Activities of Daily Living (ADLs), such as how to use a female urinal, which could be taught to women with disabilities.

During our visit, I learned that before we arrived, the hospital staff was already overwhelmed in caring for the needs of the patients. To make additional commitments to the disability community would only add additional work to an already formidable workload. We understood how potentially enormous the needs of the disability community were and the challenges of meeting those needs. However, we encouraged them to carefully evaluate the needs and their resources, and then prioritize those needs, adding more to their list as resources became available.

Dr. Raju's team seemed encouraged and believed that even small commitments could interest other health professionals to collaborate with them in providing better care for the disability community.

A Visit to the Village School

On the third day of our visit to Kachhwa, we visited one of the villages the hospital serves, which was about a 30 minute drive by car. The hospital had started a school for children who were not allowed to attend the schools in neighboring villages. This sort of exclusion occurs whenever a caste in a village does not want to mix with a different caste, especially a lower one.

The school we visited had been built four years earlier. First through eighth grades were taught in one large room, which was not large enough for all eight classes. In good weather, some of the classes were taught under

A single classroom for grades 1-8

the tree near the school building. Because of the multiple classes, teachers have to teach different curriculum, all within one room, to children at different levels and abilities. Even if there was space to separate the classes, it would still be difficult because there are too few teachers. When the classes were spread out under the trees outside, teachers would move from class to class, directing the next stage of their lessons for the day, and at the same time, keeping a watch on the rest of the students. These were gifted teachers, as they had developed their own strategies to teach the curriculum under these less than ideal circumstances, and the children seemed to be learning well.

After Jon shared his story with the students, he left the school to speak to the adults and other children who were not attending school. Meanwhile, I shared my story with the teachers and the students. The teachers informed me that there were three children that were not attending school consistently because of their disabilities. Parents were not making it a priority to bring their children to the school, believing education was not as important for them as it was for their able-bodied children.

However, two of the three children were present that day. One boy, Patrick, did not have adequate torso control, forcing him to rest one hand on the ground to keep himself upright. This made it difficult for him to write or take notes. I suggested that Patrick's teacher ask the hospital staff to create a seating system, possibly a desk with arms that would provide support on three sides, giving Patrick torso support and positional control. Patrick could then sit against the wall, with his desk in front of his body, thus having support on all four sides. This would free his hands to turn pages and write with ease.

The second student, Sheela, was partially paralyzed on one side, causing her to tilt when standing. One of her arms also appeared to be completely paralyzed, and she may have also been legally blind. I suggested that the teachers write in large print in Sheila's notebook to make it easier for her to read, and/or ask other students to help her in their free time. Bringing other students into her learning process would help them to better understand disabilities, as well as showing Sheela that she is valued by the other students.

Karen met with the parents of the two other children with disabilities, who were with the group outside the school building. Her purpose was to evaluate their physical strengths and weaknesses. One was a small boy name Troy, whose exact age was difficult to determine, though, he was old enough to be in school. The other was a very tiny 12-year old, Dolly, who we had met previously during the accessible toilet evaluation. Troy could not walk or crawl without assistance, but could bunny-hop. Dolly scooted around on her bottom. Karen taught Troy's parents two exercises to be done once a day for a specified length of time. The first exercise worked on stretching his tight inner thigh muscles. The adult was to encourage him to actively do the movements himself rather than being passively stretched by the adult. The second exercise was a squat to stand movement, teaching Troy to keep his legs in good alignment for standing (feet and knees apart). While an adult helper stood in front of Troy and provided assistance, so Troy could work on balance control using his hands/arms to help. Stepping practice took advantage of the skill gained during these exercises.

Dolly had been given a wheelchair by a donor from the United States who had previously met her. However, the chair had never been adjusted to fit her properly. The people in her area did not know how to make appropriate adaptations to the chair to meet Dolly's needs. It was not safe for Dolly to use the wheelchair at that location, because a three-foot deep water drainage canal along the narrow road between her house and the school left insufficient

room for her to independently navigate her wheelchair without the risk of rolling into the canal. While the villagers had installed a brick path for walking, the bricks were very uneven, making it very uncomfortable for a wheelchair user. Karen spent time explaining to Dolly's

Jon in front of the village school

parent's approaches for wheelchair use to encourage increased independence, not constantly pushing her wheelchair, but rather allowing Dolly the opportunity to wheel herself, discouraging other children from pushing Dolly in her wheelchair, as children are not always as careful as required. Karen recommended that providing Dolly a low to the ground rider similar to adult bikes, but low enough so she could use her arms to pedal, and installing better accommodations for toileting could help her gain more independence. The hospital staff was present to hear these explanations.

The staff discussed all they had learned, realizing for the first time the amount of assistance families of children with disabilities needed. In order to help these children and their parents, the staff recognized the need to learn more about disabilities, specifically, how to train the families in these situations and with these needs. The staff expressed appreciation for the opportunity to observe Karen using her expertise in the physical therapy field, though Karen knew that in different circumstances and with more time, she could have done more to assist the families. She noted that the father of one of the children seemed to have an instinctive ability to determine what was needed to facilitate rehabilitation, and Karen encouraged him to involve villagers with this same ability to help in the rehabilitation needs of persons with disabilities in the community. I thought our team modeled to the local team how, in the future, they could make visits in the community to evaluate the people's needs. Additionally, the team could gain ongoing expertise by inviting teams similar to ours to visit them in the future and by sending their employees for training already available through the "India Community Based Rehabilitation" (CBR) program in India.

Horrors of Fire

On our return to the hospital, its staff stopped to meet a family whose house had caught fire approximately eight months earlier. The family's son, Raj, who was in his 20's, had been badly burned after entering the burning house to rescue his nephew. He was able to save his nephew, but in the process, he had received second and third degree burns over nearly 25 percent of his body. Raj had not received proper medical treatment at the local clinic, as they were not equipped to deal with his injuries. Consequently, Raj's skin had not healed properly, and he had significant scarring. His shoulders, elbows, wrists and fingers had severe contractures, and he had lost some fingers. Because healthcare facilities are often not properly publicized in rural areas, his family was unaware of the Kachhwa hospital or the government hospital in Varanasi.

A week or two before we arrived, a hospital staff member found out about Raj and informed Dr. Raju of his condition. When Dr. Raju examined his burns, he realized that Raj needed to be taken to a hospital with a burn specialist, which he knew the family could not afford. Dr. Raju informed his staff that the only thing that could benefit Raj at this point was grafting and plastic surgery, which is very expensive. Our heart went out to Raj.

Vicky, Jon's mother, was able to encourage Raj's mother because of her own pain and experience dealing with her son's disability, and she understood firsthand what Raj's mother was going through, they both shared a similar situation and had similar feelings for their suffering sons. The hospital staff searched for a surgeon who would be willing to do the surgery free of charge. One of the staff members even traveled to meet with a surgeon in Varanasi to explain Raj's situation and condition. We as a team were amazed, yet pleased to witness the dedication the hospital staff has toward the community they serve. The day we left Kachhwa, the hospital received a call from a plastic surgeon in Varanasi who agreed to meet Raj to determine what he would be able to do to help him. This surgeon was willing to provide treatment and surgery, at no cost to the young man, if that would be a benefit to him. Though this is the story of only one of the patients we met, there are many similar stories, and the hospital staff supports the people in these stories in inspiring and extensive ways.

An Update from Kachhwa

Several months after we returned to the United States, I received the following report from Dr. Raju in which he shared further developments involving the disability community, the hospital and the local community:

- Kachhwa Christian Hospital (KCH) has set aside about 700 square feet on their campus for a Community Based Rehabilitation (CBR) Centers.

- The director of the CBR program has networked with a local disability group and a team from the hospital to assist the government in providing entitlements for their registered clients. The director has been able to help them procure 19 wheelchairs, plus crutches, calipers, bus and train passes, and disability pensions.

- The director has been working closely with their community health team, led by a medical doctor and a physiotherapist who work at a sister hospital in a nearby town. They have been supervising the director in the development of a CBR team. The physiotherapist has worked at the hospital for several years and has set up an excellent CBR program, having trained three local school leaders in CBR.

- The assembled CBR team has begun a survey of some 5,000 poor families in approximately 100 villages that the hospital serves to determine the incidence of disability among the poor, including children who are mentally challenged and those with psychiatric problems.

- The director completed training as a 'Coordinator in CBR' under the physiotherapist.

- Kachhwa hospital's ophthalmologist, who does about 2000 cataract surgeries a year, has experience in helping people with low vision. She is also trained in treating diabetic retinopathy and is establishing a low vision clinic in her department.

- Dr. Raju has been networking with an orthopedic surgeon to begin the Ponseti non-surgical management of club foot. This procedure basically involves manipulation and casting. http://en.wikipedia.org/wiki/Ponseti_Method

Most of this work was started after our visit in February 2010. I continue to be in contact with Dr Raju as these developments are taking place. He says, "We were very inspired by your visit, dedication, and desire to share the need for people with disabilities to gain independence, as well as the importance of a Biblical perspective on disability." With all these new developments, I am encouraged that by my next visit to Kachhwa, even more progress will have been made toward full inclusion of people with disabilities and their families into the life of this town.

4

New Delhi

After leaving Kachhwa, we returned to New Delhi, the capital of India. New Delhi is the twin city to Old Delhi. Together they are often simply referred to as "Delhi." Delhi is located in northern India along the banks of the Yamuna River. New Delhi and Old Delhi have a combined population of 14 million according to a 2001 Census, while New Delhi has a population of about 12 million, most of whom are Hindu. Planned by British officials

Delhi metropolitan area

prior to India's independence in 1947, Delhi is complete with paved roads, a subway system, a rail system, and air transportation. It now has a Metro system, also. Delhi is a major center of finance and commerce and is home to the Presidential Palace. Embassies from around the world are based there. Public-sector jobs are the primary source of employment in the capital. The large number of English-speaking workers has attracted international companies to Delhi in recent years, resulting in a growing service sector.

Government-sponsored programs encourage employment of persons with disabilities and women in particular. Unfortunately many people in the disability community are isolated, due to mental and physical barriers that prevent them from being accepted in their communities. An example of a government program is the Indira Gandhi National Disability Pension Scheme (IGNDPS), which provides assistance to persons with disabilities between the ages of 18 and 64 years of age living in poverty through a financial pension of 200 Rupees monthly from the central government and 200 Rupees from the state government. (http://india.gov.in/govt/view scheme.php?schemeid=1866) Also, The Rehabilitation Council of India Ministry regulates the training policies, programs, and healthcare facilities for physically and mentally challenged citizens of India, and includes the District Rehabilitation Center (DRC) Project, Regional Rehabilitation Training Center (RRTC), and National Information Center on Disability & Rehabilitation (NICDR). (http://india.gov.in/citizen/health/rehabilitation. php). The National Handicapped Finance & Development Corporation provides financial assistances to persons with disabilities with the purpose of self reliance and economic productivity, such as soft loans for small businesses. (http://www.disabilityindia.org/govtrehab.cfm). The government provides financial assistance to organizations in rural and urban areas who work with the rehabilitation of people with leprosy; such as awareness generation programs that focus on early intervention, educational and vocational training, economic rehabilitation, and social integration. The government also provides assistance in the establishment and development of special disability-focused schools for those with orthopedic, hearing and speech, visual, and mental disabilities. (http://www.disabilityindia.org/aidscheme. cfm).

The Indian government census estimates that there are over a quarter million people in Delhi living with severe and profound disabilities. Conditions that do not involve physical, cognitive, or sensory impairment or conditions that are only mild-to-moderate are not tracked. Disability is still stigmatized in India, particularly in the educational sphere. Teachers in India are not generally required to go through any special training to work with special needs children, as teachers are in the United States, though special training is available for those who are interested. Most persons in India know very little about the cause of disabilities, what people with disabilities are capable of doing, or how people with disabilities can be assisted.

http://www.mapsofindia.com/delhi/population-of-new-delhi.html

http://www.exploredelhi.com/history-of-delhi.html

http://delhitourism.nic.in/delhitourism/aboutus/index.jsp

http://delhitourism.nic.in/delhitourism/aboutus/history_of_delhi.jsp

Because of this stigma, I was thrilled at the invitation to speak to primary and secondary school students about disability awareness in New Delhi. In addition, our schedule included a week-long visit with patients at the India Spinal Injury Center (ISIC), to encourage the patients who were undergoing physical therapy. Consequently, our time in New Delhi would be far more relaxed than our earlier visits to the other cities in India. However, as the days passed, our time was quickly filled up with many opportunities to visit churches, organizations and individuals to share about disability and its effects on the families.

India Spinal Injury Center (ISIC)

Vicky was a familiar face to many of the therapists at ISIC, because it was the facility where her son, Jon, received his initial treatment after his accident, prior to being transferred to the United States. Both Jon and Vicky had good rapport with the staff. The social worker informed the therapists about our visit, so they knew what to expect as Vicky moved around the Center, speaking with the patients during their therapy sessions.

I had first met the staff at ISIC in 2009, when they had invited me to conduct a workshop for the patients and staff. The subject I shared with them was, "How to Treat Your Caregivers." I chose this topic because, in India, nearly all caregivers for persons with disabilities are family members.

Many times, I have personally witnessed the stress and burdens placed on caregivers.

In 2010, my role was speaking one-on-one with ISIC patients to encourage them, which was very different from giving a workshop. Initially, it felt like a "cold call," because I had never met any of the patients before. But after talking to a few of them, I began to feel more at ease and welcomed by them. I also had the sense that other patients and their family members were watching me, hoping that I would visit with them, too. Following are the stories of few of the patients I visited.

Balbeer's Story

I noticed a young lady in her 30's who smiled pleasantly at me each time I looked toward her. When her therapy ended, the therapist transferred her carefully into her wheelchair, and the young lady wheeled herself toward me with great effort. She introduced herself as Balbeer. From our conversation, I learned that she had two children who she had left at home with relatives, while her husband and mother-in-law remained with her at the hospital during her therapy. This was because the family lived in a different town, a great distance from New Delhi. Balbeer was very fortunate to have such a supportive husband and in-laws because in India there are many stories of wives with disabilities who have quite different outcomes. More often than not, when the wife becomes disabled, her husband and her in-laws choose to abandon her.

Joy encouraging Balbeer

Balbeer's story began while she was hanging clothes on the clothesline, and she lost her balance, fell backwards, and hit her spine on the high curb. It saddened me to realize that a simple fall had taken away her mobility and forced her to use a wheelchair for an indefinite period of time. It was providential that even though she was 70 percent paralyzed from her waist down, her arms were unharmed. The doctors and therapists were hopeful that, with intensive therapy, Balbeer would one day walk again, albeit with the assistance of crutches or a walker. For the time being, the Spinal Center staff wanted to teach Balbeer to function from her wheelchair, and that greatly discouraged her. However, I explained that I lived alone and was able to accomplish everything from my wheelchair, which seemed to give her hope and encouragement, bringing a huge smile to her face.

Tera's Story

I continued making visitation rounds in the hospital's physical therapy department. It was a large area with several types of standard physical conditioning equipment arranged around the room and extending from the ceiling. I noticed an elderly woman named Tera sitting motionless in front of a pulley machine. A young man was pleading with her to use the machine to strengthen her arm muscles. He seemed discouraged and helpless, because he was unable to convince Tera that there were benefits to her therapy treatment. The doctors had recommended that she exercise her muscles ten to fifteen minutes several times a day, but Tera refused, having seen little improvement from her previous efforts. I asked her in the local Hindi language, "Grandma, how are you? Are you too tired to exercise?" "Grandma" is a form of address that is part of the Indian culture. Older people are not addressed by their given name, but rather, terms such as sir, madam, grandma, grandpa, aunty, uncle, brother, or sister are used.

Tera responded, "No, it is not worth it, plus I am old and will die soon." In reality, she may have been right, but I would not let her give up so easily. Continuing, I said, "As far as being old is concerned, your age does not give you a ticket to die soon. It is not up to anyone to decide someone's birth or death. You may still have a long life, so wouldn't you want to live as independently as possible? Even though I have lived in a wheelchair all my life and I may have many more years left, I know I want to live the rest of my life as independently as possible." When Tera learned that I had lived all my life in a wheelchair and will be for the rest of my life, she softened, tears forming in her eyes, "I have only been in a wheelchair a few months and have already improved much. The doctors are saying I may not walk, but my arms can get stronger." I shared that because my arms are stronger, I can do many things for myself. In the end, Tera assured me that she would try harder, and even gave me a hug. The young man, who was her son, had recorded our entire conversation on his phone and promised that every time her motivation waned, he would replay it. We laughed and said our goodbyes.

Rachel's Story

Jon and Vicki had known Rachel for four years. She was admitted at ISIC at the same time Jon had been. Rachel had made great progress since that time and was now learning how to transfer herself independently using a transfer board. Since I also use a transfer board and Jon had used one before, we encouraged her with some suggestions as she practiced.

Rachel had to withdraw from school, as the school was not willing to accommodate her special needs. She lost all her school friends. Making the situation worse, her family neglected to take her access needs into consideration as they reconstructed their house, moving the main part of the house to the second floor. The change made it even more difficult for Rachel to enter and exit the house. This story underscores the attitude many Indian families have toward people with disabilities, viewing them as unimportant due to the fact that they will not be as productive in life as their nondisabled family members.

Since our team was volunteering at ISIC that week, we were given comfortable accommodations at their guesthouse, a fully furnished two-bedroom apartment. Each bedroom had an attached bathroom. Jon's wheelchair was significantly smaller than mine, so no changes were needed for him. However, my chair was wider and could not fit through the bathroom door. When we informed the maintenance people about this issue, they immediately came and removed the bathroom door, providing just enough clearance to enter the bathroom. To ensure privacy, the bedroom door would have to be closed. The guesthouse also had a full kitchen with a refrigerator, toaster, microwave, electric tea kettle, and stove. We felt very much at home. Personally, I experienced independence, because the apartment itself was fairly accessible.

Our primary focus at the ISIC was to encourage patients. On our first Sunday in New Delhi, Karen and I attended Pastor Ernie's and his wife, Marian's, church where I had been invited to speak. The congregation was primarily a college and career age group. I shared my story, noting from the Scriptures that our responsibility is to reach out to the people with disabilities and their families. The message was well received, so I left with the hope that the foundation had been laid for future disability ministry in this church.

As I shared during the service, a young man named John seemed touched by my personal story and the Scriptures about trusting in God. His father, Dr. William, and his mother are co-founders of Mount Carmel schools. Mount Carmel has three branches in two buildings. They are the most influential Christian schools in New Delhi. As soon as the service ended, John contacted his father by phone to ask him to invite me to speak at one or both of Mount Carmel's schools. John informed me that as soon as he was able to talk with his father and get his confirmation, he would call me with his father's answer. Finally, after a day of waiting, John called and said I was invited to speak in an assembly at the first school, where his father was the principal.

Mount Carmel

On Wednesday morning, John picked up Karen and me. I was scheduled to speak at the beginning of the school day at the 8:00 a.m. chapel. The school building was a very large, three story building. There were six to eight steps leading up to the ground floor, so two men had to carry my wheelchair up those steps. Once inside, there was an elevator for easy access to the upper levels. The building was beautifully designed, similar to a modern American school. The walls were decorated with paintings of India and Scripture from the Bible. Upon arrival, John introduced us to his father and a few school

Speaking to 2,500 students (first school)

administrators. I did not realize how large the student body was until I was ready to speak and saw all their faces looking up at me, all beautifully dressed in burgundy and white uniforms.

Later, I learned that the school enrollment was about 2,500 students in grades kindergarten through 12th grade.

I spoke in English without an interpreter, as they were taught in the English language. I shared my story as to how I had become disabled, and how my faith has motivated me through my life struggles. I also encouraged the students to reach out to people with disabilities and befriend them. After the chapel service, we were introduced to a few teachers. Karen and I were invited to breakfast with Dr. William in his office, which was very elegant

Breakfast with Dr. William

and the furniture was nicely situated around the room. Upon entering the office, to my right was a sitting area with a large sofa and two chairs surrounding a silk rug with a glass coffee table in the center. In the adjacent corner, was Dr. William's large L-shaped desk, holding his computer, fax machine, printer, and

the telephone. Lastly between his desk and the door, was a long conference table, massive and larger than I would have expected.   We all sat around one end of the conference table as Dr. William shared his powerful story of deciding to follow Christ. Even though he was raised in a Christian family, he had not been a devout Christian. Later in life, however, he made the decision to become a true follower of Christ. Dr. William added that he has never regretted that decision. Following our meal, he invited me to return the next day to speak at the second school.

On Thursday morning, Karen and I traveled to the second school, where Dr. William's wife was the principal, and we spoke to approximately 2,500 students. Again, speaking in English, I shared my story and challenged the students to help other students and other neighborhood children with disabilities by treating them with respect. I also encouraged them to recognize the potential in children with disabilities, as they have gifts and talents, as well. All that was needed was assistance in developing those gifts.

Speaking to 2,500 students (2nd school)

After speaking, Karen and I joined Mrs. William for breakfast. It was a wonderful time of fellowship, and we were greatly blessed as she introduced us to the school staff. From there, Karen and I rotated between classes of students where we presented for forty-five minutes in each classroom. Not expecting this kind of opportunity, we were not prepared with a slide presentation or an agenda, but Karen and I had experience being spontaneous. Initially, we explained basic disabilities and how these disabilities necessitate dependence on other people.

Training students with disability

We added that every effort should be made to help these individuals become as independent as possible. We also described different disabilities in greater detail and were able to provide suggestions on how the students at this school could help those around them who have disabilities.

Continuing Training at Mount Caramel

In the classroom, we were given complete freedom over the training and presentations. Each class was different. Some groups were quiet and the students were shy, while others were interactive, the students asking many questions. Several students shared that they had family members with disabilities, and as a result of our presentations, they realized that, if these family members had the right assistance, they could be more independent. I emphasized the importance of encouraging people with disabilities toward more independence and how to best handle various situations when assisting, as they arise.

For example, Jack, one of the students, described a boy named Danny, who lived in his neighborhood and had an intellectual disability. Jack wanted to befriend him, but other boys in the neighborhood terrorized Danny, calling him crazy and bullying him. Jack was teased, too, for being nice to Danny. I encouraged Jack to continue being nice to Danny, and explained to the class what cognitive disabilities were, their implications, and how ridiculing anyone is the same as ridiculing God, the Creator of us all. It was amazing that every class closely attended to our presentations. Karen and I spent the entire school day with these students. After normal school hours, Mt. Carmel offers schooling for students whose parents are unable to afford the school's tuition. I was asked to speak to this group the following day. There were about 200 students in grades first through eighth. Two of the students had disabilities. I used this reality to encourage a discussion about the fact that, even though some students struggled with memorization or writing, it did not mean they were unable to learn. They simply had a different way of processing information. This required either a different method of teaching/learning for these students in

Speaking to 200 students (3rd school)

order for them to understand the same lessons, or a slower pace of presenting material to learn the concepts. I spoke in Hindi, which is their first language.

Continuing Training in New Delhi

While we were in New Delhi, we provided a disability ministry conference. It was a short, two hour conference, but it provided us an opportunity to visit with local pastors and community leaders. We cast the "vision" for disability ministry by sharing with the group why we do what we do and explaining what the Bible says about serving people with disabilities. Even though the disability conference was the first effort of its kind in the city, those who attended left wanting to do more to assist the disability community there. Some expressed that it was the first time they had attended a conference about helping people with disabilities. Prior to our trip, Vicky had spent several weeks organizing this conference. Upon arrival, we met with local community leaders and pastors to discuss the final planning and presentation of the conference. Everything was in place and confirmed for the 60 people who would attend. The conference attracted people from different professional backgrounds, including clergy, medical professionals, medical students, social workers, community workers and assistive technology specialists. Because the audience was primarily Christian, we discussed disability and strategies for reaching out from a Christian perspective. By the end of the conference, everyone agreed that they desired to do something to empower the disability community in New Delhi. We were hopeful that another disability conference could be held in the future with some of these same people assisting with the planning.

Women's Group

Vicki made arrangements for me to meet with a group of Christian women from various churches who meet weekly for Bible study and prayer. Vicky had initially met them while Jon was admitted to the ISIC. This women's group visited with Jon, Vicky and her husband at the hospital to pray for them and encourage them. These women were the support that Jon and his parents needed while Jon was in the Hospital in India. After Jon's initial treatment, he was brought back to the United States for continued treatment and therapy.

Once Jon's treatment and therapy was completed, he and Vicky started travelling back to India to conduct workshops for quadriplegics and to reconnect with the friends they had made during Jon's stay at the hospital in New Delhi. During these trips Jon and Vicky communicated with the women's group the needs of their friends with quadriplegia, especially the need for wheelchairs. These women started praying and encouraging these friends with quadriplegia and joined Vicki and Jon in this project to raise part of the funds for wheelchairs needed by their friends and acquaintances with quadriplegia.

I was invited to share my story and teach a Bible study with this women's group. Our hostess, Vini, drove Karen, Vicki, and me to her house, similar in appearance to a townhouse. Upon entering a small living room, we were greeted by 25 members of the group who were waiting for us. Beginning, I shared a passage of Scripture from the Bible, followed by the story of my disability. I shared about how at four months of age, I contracted Polio, leaving me paralyzed from my shoulders to my toes. The doctors informed my parents that I would not live beyond five years, and if I did live, I would be in a vegetative state for the rest of my life. One doctor even stated that he could not bring life into a dead thing, referring to me. Visiting several doctors and getting little help, my parents decided to pray, fast, and trust in God. After my dad fasted and prayed for two weeks, I wiggled one little toe. That was just the beginning of God's answer to my parent's prayers. From that point on, I continued to improve ever so slowly, until now I function very independently. Except for having to use a wheelchair, I am able to live on my own and can do most things for myself with minimal assistance. When I chose the field of disability as a profession, it was not because of my own disability, but rather, my having lived with disability has helped me understand and empathize with the disability of others.

I concluded by expressing excitement and encouragement for the efforts of these women in reaching out to people with disabilities, choosing to visit patients with disabilities in the hospital and raising part of the money needed to purchase wheelchairs for a couple of people affected by disability. The women were challenged to invite more women into their group who could partner with them, so that more people with disabilities could be reached. I encouraged them to continue their pursuit of finding new and specific ways to help people with disabilities. After sharing my story, the ladies had arranged a grand potluck lunch. The large dining table was heaped with a variety of Indian dishes, including various types of curries, meats, and vegetables cooked with spices. There was also a dip made with yogurt, seasoned with spices, and other homemade appetizers. The whole house was redolent with the aroma of a sumptuous home cooked meal. To say the least, it was a memorable meeting.

Postscript

Several months after returning from my trip to India, Pastor Ernie's wife, Marian, a co-pastor with her husband at this particular church, visited Chicago. We met and discussed ways in which we could develop and expand the disability ministry in New Delhi. It was decided that Marian needed to communicate with the college and career group at their church who are interested in serving the disability community. After her return to India, she and her husband challenged their church to reach out and serve those with disabilities. Since then, I have been receiving emails from some of those young people desiring to learn about training opportunities in disability ministry. From these communications, the possibility now exists of holding a disability ministry training during my next trip to Delhi.

5

Hubli

Karen and I were excited to travel to Hubli once again, via Mumbai. Hubli, the twin city of Dharwad, is located in the state of Karnataka and is a rapidly growing city of 900,000 people. In ancient history, Hubli was known as Raya Hubli or Pubballi, meaning "old village," and originally consisted of nine separate villages which have now all become Hubli-Dharwad. Under Vijayanagara Rayas, an emperor in the Vijayanagara Empire from 1336 to 1646 CE, the city flourished as an industrial town, producing cotton, saltpeter, and iron. This industrial tradition has continued to the present day with industries that produce machine tools, steel furniture, food products, rubber, and leather goods. Hubli-Dharwad is second in size only to Bangalore and boasts of many tourist attractions, such as beautiful monasteries, mosques, Unkal Lake, and the beautiful palace made entirely of glass, known as the Glass House.

The literacy rate in Hubli-Dharwar is about 72.1 percent. Poverty predominates, as one in four people live in the slums and forty percent of those living in the slums live below the poverty line. Only one in four families has clean drinking water. Many children are born underdeveloped, due to the inability of the family to pay for medical care. The lack of sufficient services can also be seen in the disregard for the needs of the disabled. At a recent protest, people with disabilities held signs calling for safer passages, ramps for the buses and trains, and accessible infrastructure in the city.

While I enjoy visiting Hubli, there are still many difficulties associated with traveling in general for those that use a wheelchair. Airports have a predetermined set of rules and procedures for aiding people with disabilities. However, they are very limited and leave no room for input from the disabled individual with disabilities or their travel companion, information that would make the whole process easier for disabled travelers with disabilities, as well as the airport and the airline personnel assisting them. Each time I fly, it is a battle to get on and off the plane. It's both frustrating and entertaining as I repeatedly try to explain why their procedure will not work for me and that I know this from past experience. Each time I travel, I try to educate the airport and the airline employees on ways to help people with disabilities when they travel. For example, each traveler with disability has different needs, and only that individual or the traveling companion knows the physical limitations and how best the person can be assisted. It is important for the airport or airline staff to ask him/her how he/she can assist in transferring the person from a wheelchair to the aisle chair or from aisle chair to the plane seat, and not grabbing the person in trying to assist. Sometimes helping in a wrong way can become more of a hindrance than not helping at all.

Traveling within the United States is a totally different experience for those with disabilities. When traveling within the United States, I use my battery powered scooter, which can transport me easily from my home to the accessible van and directly into the airport. At the check-in counter, I receive assistance up to the gate. When boarding the plane, I use my transfer board (which travels everywhere with me) for an easy shift from the wheelchair to the aisle chair and from the aisle chair to the aisle seat of the plane. The arm rest on a certain number of aisle seats can be pulled back for easier transfer. The staff is knowledgeable and will listen to instructions as to how to better assist me. This practice allows me to transfer safely and independently, which is empowering for all with a disability.

The airplanes to Hubli are the smallest I have ever flown in, with only twenty seats. It is amazing that air travel employees at the Hubli airport know what to do to assist passengers with disabilities and are willing to listen, even though the city is smaller in comparison to Varanasi or New Delhi. This is due, in part, to my many previous visits in and out of this airport, so many times, in fact, that they now recognize me. The most frightening part of traveling to and

Carry on chair not for aircraft aisles

from an airport without a large terminal is being strapped in the narrow aisle chair and carried up and down the twelve steps to the plane. Some of the carry-on chairs are the correct width to pass down the aisles of the plane and are the same height as the seats of the plane. They also provide wider carry-on chairs, but they are unable to pass down the aisle. These wider chairs work well for those who can stand and walk a few steps to the seat. However, since I cannot stand or walk, the wider ones do not work for me. Both types of chairs are available at each airport, but ironically, the airport staff never provides the right chair the first time, and they attempt to convince me that it will work. It is an ordeal for me to transfer from the small aisle chair, because it is significantly lower than my wheelchair. The assistants try to help by pulling my arm, but my body never moves an inch from the seat, as I talk louder and louder, asking them to release my arm. I patiently explain, once again, that it is not working and it will not work. At Hubli, they actually brought the right chair the first time.

When we finally arrived in Hubli, my wheelchair was unloaded first. Karen exited the plane first, so she could assemble my wheelchair, and then she returned to the plane to assist me in transferring into the small aisle chair. The four male airport staff carefully carried me down the steps of the plane, and as they tilted the chair backwards in preparation to descend the steps, I noticed a concerned expression on Karen's face. She saw the fear in my eyes, as she witnessed the process. Thankfully, I arrived safely on the ground. Once in my wheelchair, I experienced relief, and finally felt "like myself" again. I was pushed by one of the airport staff into the airport and requested my baggage claim tickets, so that my luggage could be retrieved. I thanked the young man, using his first name. He did not realize that I had read it on his name tag and replied, "Ah, you remember my name!" "Yeah," I responded, "I see you every time I come here!" It was true that I had recognized his face. He added, "I help so many people every day, but no one remembers my name. I am so pleased!" I was blessed to be able to "make his day."

While I was waiting for my luggage, I could see the Operation Equip India (OEI) team waiting for us outside the airport. Tommy, the director of international teams, and his wife, Cindy, were closest to the door. As we exited the baggage claim, we were greeted with hugs and garlands. It was great to see this young married couple, because on my previous trip, they were not even engaged. Standing behind Tommy and Cindy were the director and his wife and a few other staff members. We loaded

Wheelchair accessible van

the accessible van, and I was relieved that I didn't need to be concerned about transferring in and out of my wheelchair again. The van had four point tie downs and a bar which passes through the two big wheels, preventing the wheelchair from moving. Also, there was a seat belt and harness to prevent me from sliding off the wheelchair seat.

We drove for about thirty minutes through the crowded roads on the outskirts of Hubli to the OEI center. From a distance, I noticed a new gate to the OEI center, painted an eye-catching yellow. As the driver drew closer to the building, I saw the students and staff members waiting to welcome us.

It was exciting to see this new group of students, though I was already missing the students I had worked with on my previous two visits. We were escorted to the same room that had been prepared for me on previous visits, which had an attached accessible bathroom. Even when I am not there, they still refer to the room as "Joy's room." This time, however, we even had our own armoire (portable closet) with a lock. This provision was a welcomed convenience, as we would not have to lock our room every time we left. Since many outsiders visit the OEI campus, our belongings needed to be safely locked up. We visited a little bit, briefly reviewing our plans, and then said our "goodbyes" to the staff. Karen and I were anxious to unpack our luggage and change our clothes to enjoy some time of rest.

History and work of Operation Equip India (OEI):

OEI was started in Hubli in 1997, by Tim and Aruna Swauger, with the goal of equipping India's disabled community with the physical, educational and socio-economic tools necessary for a life of independence and advancement. The organization grew very quickly and began making a significant difference in the lives of the young people with disabilities in Hubli and the surrounding villages. Over the past thirteen years, the original staff grew from two people to forty. Some of OEI's programs include outreach to leprosy survivors, corrective surgeries, physical rehabilitation and community-based rehabilitation. OEI built a large hostel (dormitory) facility to use for the physical rehabilitation programs and for students pursuing their education at the local colleges, universities and vocational training programs.

The hostel is a safe place for youth with disabilities who are from rural areas. The length of their stays ranges from a short time, several months to even two years or more, being determined by their need and into which program they are accepted. So far OEI provides full scholarships to all students to complete their education. This funding pays for room, meals, tuition, books and other school supplies.

OEI operates a handicraft training and production unit which trains young women and men. Here they make different handicrafts, training them in a trade which will provide an income. After completing the training, they can work for the Handicraft department from their homes. OEI gives them an order and provides them with the raw material for the products with a deadline to complete the work. When the completed products are delivered, the workers receive the payment for their labor. They can also use their skills to earn more income by working in the community or by working for other organizations. The leprosy project operated by OEI provides care and surgeries for persons affected by this debilitating disease. OEI works with several leprosy colonies at one time. In 2007, OEI launched another initiative to raise awareness and equip the nearly 3.1 million people living with HIV/AIDS, six percent of whom live in Hubli's twin city of Dharwad.

There are two floors in the OEI dorm that can accommodate about 45 students with disabilities. The ground floor houses females and the first floor houses males. The OEI staff visits the villages to meet with families impacted by disability and to inform them about the resources available at OEI. Availability of funding dictates how many students are accepted into their various programs. The majority of the families cannot afford an education for a child with a disability, so, whatever resources the family does have are invested into the education of their able-bodied children. After a careful evaluation process to determine the student's potential for a college education or vocational training, a decision is made whether or not to admit the student to the program, again depending on the funding available. Once accepted, he/she lives at the OEI dorm and attends nearby colleges. Upon completing their education, the students return to their villages to find work with assistance from OEI, as needed. Some students find employment within their community, some go outside their village for work, and some are even hired by OEI.

My relationship with OEI

I became acquainted with OEI through my travels with Wheels for the World (WFTW) which is a part of the ministry of Joni and Friends. OEI partners with WFTW to distribute hundreds of wheelchairs and other mobility devices to persons with disabilities from Hubli and the surrounding villages. Over the years, during the wheelchair distribution outreaches, the OEI staffs have observed my counseling and advising clients and individuals and families impacted by disability. As a result, OEI invited me to assist them with the church leadership training and by supporting staff and students with disabilities.

This was a mutually beneficial partnership for both OEI and me. Since I grew up with a disability in India, understand the culture, and am fluent in some Indian languages and dialects, my assistance would be invaluable. Since 2008, I have been working with OEI several weeks at a time during my trips to India. I also helped them while home in the United States. These efforts included providing advice and support for improving the training material for disability ministry instruction for their church leadership. Karen had also volunteered her time to work alongside me to help the OEI staff in editing these training materials. I also provided advice on meeting the various needs of OEI clients and mentoring and supporting their staff. This was my third trip separate from WFTW to serve the disability community in collaboration with OEI. It has been a privilege getting to know their leadership, staff, students and other clients. OEI is staffed with quality people who are truly compassionate in their efforts to enhance the lives of the people with disabilities in the community. Even though there are other organizations in Hubli serving those with disability, none are as effective as OEI in empowering young people with disabilities.

After attending devotions with the students on our first day, Karen and I ate with the students in the dining room. Since we were guests, we were served different food than the students were. Normally, students eat rice, lentils, beans, vegetables, and chapatti, plain tortilla- type bread, with some yogurt, a pickle, or salad on the side. For us, they cooked fried bread, other vegetarian delicacies, eggs, noodles, soup, and desserts. When we offered these special dishes to the students they would politely refuse. If we insisted, they would move away from us, so we stopped offering them our food. Since most of the students were vegetarians, either because of their faith or because of the economic situations of their families, OEI served only vegetarian food. This eliminates the possibility of offending any of the students. With the exception of eggs, non-vegetarian food is not cooked in OEI's kitchen. Although all of our team members were non-vegetarians and not used to strict vegetarian diet, we all enjoyed the food and clearly understood the cultural reasoning behind it.

The following morning, we ate breakfast with the vocational students, though some of them had already left to attend classes at various schools, colleges or universities. Students in India, including those at OEI, do not use the term 'school' if they are attending a college or university, unlike here in the United States.

At nine o'clock, the staff arrived to join together for devotions. For the staff, having devotions before starting work, is part of the OEI culture. Afterwards, we met with Tommy to review the details of the program for our remaining three weeks with OEI. To our surprise, Karen learned that she was being asked to present more than she had prepared for. Seeing the panic on her face, Tommy tried to encourage her with the words, "Not to worry, we'll give you an office and a computer and a lock in the door, so that you will have time to prepare." It was not as encouraging to Karen as he had hoped, since the center has only dial-up access to the Internet, making it difficult to do research, and she had not brought many resources with her.

OEI has many departments, each providing a different service to the disability community. These services will be discussed in greater detail in the following chapter.

The day after our orientation, we met with the director of the Friends department, which provides counseling and spiritual direction, as needed, to the students. While we always had a general understanding of what this department does, knowing more details gave Karen and I added respect for the organization and its staff in their commitment to serving people with disabilities. We ate lunch with the departmental staff and gained a better understanding of the role of each staff member. After lunch, we were free to rest or spend time with the students and staff to offer our help, where needed. We decided to spend most of our free time with the staff members.

The next morning, Karen and I attended the staff devotions led by one of the female staff from the Friends department. After devotions, we met with the Central Karnataka Spiritual Enrichment Program (CKSEP) team to discuss the material for each session for the Disability Ministry Training Seminar. We spent time fine tuning the PowerPoint presentation for the upcoming training seminar. CKSEP had already planned Disability Ministry Training for the church leadership in three different Districts in the State of Karnataka. A separate chapter talks about the trainings in those three districts. After updating the material for CKSEP trainings, we met with OEI's Community Based Rehabilitation (CBR) department to learn about the many ministries they provide in the community.

On Saturday, the OEI driver took Karen and me to the director's house for lunch. He lives in a third floor condo, which presented a problem for me, because the elevator started on the floor above ground level. Again, I had to be carried in my wheelchair up a flight of stairs to the first floor. The previous year, I had to be carried up three flights of stairs, because the elevator had not yet been installed. I was more concerned for the safety of those carrying my wheelchair than I was for my own. Unfortunately, the elevator was not

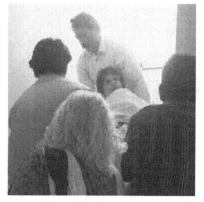

Joy being carried up a flight of stairs

wheelchair accessible, and we questioned the advantage of starting an elevator one floor above the entrance to the building. Fortunately, my wheelchair narrowly fit through the elevator door. I learned that the director and others were not concerned about the non-accessibility of the elevator, because they had carried me to the third floor in previous years.

In India, hospitality is a very important part of their culture, and Indians go out of their way to show generosity and warmth to their guests, both people they know well and care for, as well as to those who they may not know very well. Finally, we arrived at the director's condo, greeted with a sumptuous aroma of the meal his wife, an incredible cook, had prepared for us. It was the first time since leaving the United States that we had eaten fresh fruit in a home. For safety reasons, we had avoided fresh fruit or salads, due to the different strains of bacteria that were present in India but not in the United States. Graciously, they had rinsed the fruit once with salt water and then again with filtered water. Following a delicious lunch, we spent the afternoon discussing what OEI had accomplished since my last visit in 2009. We relaxed talking and playing with their two daughters, who were ages nine and two. Also, access to internet offered us the opportunity to read and respond to our emails.

Later that same evening, we ate dinner with Pearl, another OEI staff member. In 2008, when Karen and I had been in Hubli, Karen had taught the staff about prenatal care. At that time, Pearl was pregnant with her first child, so she listened intently to what Karen shared and applied what she had learned to her pregnancy and upcoming childbirth. That same year, I had counseled Pearl regarding some personal and family issues, and she reported how helpful that had been. Her first child was now a beautiful 18 month old girl, and Pearl was expecting her second child. During our current visit, Karen and I met her husband and extended family for the first time.

Pearl prepared a traditional Karnataka vegetarian meal. Her family chided her for choosing to make such simple dishes for her western friends, but Pearl was confident we would enjoy her cooking. Everything was delicious and very different from the Indian food we had had at other locations during our travels. That is the beauty of India. It has many states, and each state has its own variety of food, style, colors, clothing and jewelry. Karen and I had a wonderful time visiting with this beautiful family and partaking in their gracious hospitality.

The next day was Sunday, and we went to an accessible church with a couple of the staff members. The pastor's focus is reaching out to people with disabilities and making them feel comfortable in his congregation. This particular Sunday I was just visiting, but in previous years I had spoken at this church during my visits. I had shared my life story and the biblical view on disability, though it had not been one of the churches where I had provided disability ministry training. The majority of the people were from a middle class background, and a few individuals and families have been impacted by disabilities.

The following day, Tommy and I trained some of the staff about accountability, in terms of time management and accessing the hierarchy of authority when problems arise. It was basically a round table discussion. We also presented a couple of skits on this topic, followed by a brief teaching and discussion time.

Karen and I, as well as some of the OEI staff, were excited in anticipation of Amanda and Hannah's arrival. They had arrived in India the day before and had spent the night in New Delhi with the Pastor Ernie and his wife, Mariane. It can be a bit unnerving travelling to a new country and not knowing the language, the culture, or what to expect. After picking Amanda and Hannah from the airport and on our return to OEI, the staff bought some Western food, in case Amanda or Hannah could not eat the Indian food at the Center. Arriving at the Center, we enjoyed tea and coffee together and settled the young ladies in their room.

Before eating dinner, we introduced Hannah and Amanda to the students who were living at the OEI hostel (dorm). The students were excited to meet them, but some were a bit shy as they could not communicate in English. Amanda and Hannah wanted to learn about the students, as well, but the language difference was a huge barrier. The heavy Indian/American accents of the speakers made the English words difficult to understand for both language speakers, but the smiles on their faces indicated that it did not matter.

Some of my time was dedicated to meeting and counseling with the OEI students individually.

Penny was the first student I met. She had almost completed her vocational training in stitching and embroidering. Penny dreaded the prospect of returning home where she had been physically and verbally abused by her family because of her disability. They considered Penny's disability a curse and a burden to the family. As a self-protection, she had started using vulgar language, and the OEI staff had helped her realize that this behavior was not helping her relationship with her family. Now that Penny had accepted her disability and knew she was worthy in God's eyes, Penny asked me how she should expect to be treated by other people. Her questions included, "What will I do if my family still treats me the same way?" Her family had already told her that if she did not bring home income, then they did not want her to return home. I shared with Penny that part of the reason she was given the opportunity to be trained at OEI was so she could work and receive an income. She was encouraged to contract with OEI to become a home worker and then explain to her family how this income will be partially shared with them. Additionally, Penny needed to explain to her family how her work needed to be completed in a timely manner, so that she would be provided with more work. Penny needed to have time to complete each project, and therefore, would not be able to do all the cooking and cleaning, as she had done in past. Penny also needed a small work area in the house to keep her work supplies safe and out of the way of the household activity. If the supplies become damaged or dirty, Penny would have to pay to replace the supplies.

Penny also was reminded not to treat her family the way they treated her. She was encouraged to treat them the same way she wanted to be treated. Lastly, I advised Penny the need to keep in contact with the OEI staff to keep them current as to what is happening in her life. If her circumstances did not improve, perhaps the OEI staff could assist by talking with Penny's family or helping her locate another place to live.

Judy, a day student, arrived with her teenage daughter, Lisa. Judy was in tears, because Lisa was skipping school, and to avoid attending, was hiding in the homes of either a neighbor or a relative. Judy was very concerned about her daughter's future. She had punished Lisa, but felt guilty for doing so. Lisa sat quietly and listened, as her mother poured out her heart to me through an interpreter. I asked Lisa to sit next to me, so I could speak to her in simple English. This gave her a sense of privacy, since her mother did not speak or understand English. She shared from her heart. She explained that some students at school had been teasing Lisa and she had no friends. Whenever she made friends, others gossiped about her, and she would subsequently lose her new friend. I suspected that there must be some family history or background the students knew about. I assured Lisa that we were talking as friends, and anything she shared would not be used to hurt her in any way.

Later that day, I learned that both of Lisa's parents had HIV/AIDS, which helped me to understand some of Judy's irritation, concern, and anger towards her daughter. It also became apparent that the students teased the young eighth grader because of the stigma attached to HIV/AIDS. However, a week later, Judy shared with me that her daughter had not missed a day of class since she and I had talked together.

On the first Sunday morning after Amanda and Hannah had arrived, we attended church together. Some of the students from the hostel attended this church. Following the church service, we joined Rodni, an OEI staff member, and his wife at their home to eat lunch. At that time, Rodni was a story writer for OEI, writing background stories about prospective students and clients in order to place them on a waiting list for available funding. We, as a team, visited with Rodni, while his wife finished cooking, and then we were served lunch. Often in the Indian culture, the host and hostess eat after the guests have eaten and left. At other times, the male members of the family eat with the guest, and the women eat afterwards. Though we very much wanted to eat with both Rodni and his wife, unfortunately, they decided to serve us and eat later. The meal was delicious, consisting of fried rice with fresh peas, chicken curry, homemade yogurt, and a salad of cucumber, carrots, tomatoes and onions on the side. I was concerned that Amanda and Hannah would not be able to eat the food served to us, especially since Amanda was not used to spicy food. However, I was amazed, as well as pleased, to watch her as she took a second and third helping, thoroughly enjoying the food. We all knew that, according to the culture, we were not to leave food on the plate, so we were all trying to finish our food, while making certain we were not served any more food. Often the moment guests finish what is on the plate, the hostess would fill the plate again, sometimes without asking, and guests are forced to overeat only out of courtesy to the hostess. Consequently, I had warned Amanda and Hannah that if their plate is empty and someone comes to fill it again, they should cover their plate with one hand and keep it there until their host stops insisting.

After lunch, Rodni and his wife offered us tea and dessert, but we politely declined. We spent the afternoon, listening to their favorite music, which was in both English and their local language. After our time of good fellowship, we left so that Rodni and his wife could eat their lunch. We returned to the OEI Center to rest, as Amanda and Hannah were still experiencing jetlag and needed a nap.

Over the weekend, OEI staff members take the opportunity to spend time with the students in the dorm, often playing games with them. Sometimes they play board games, but when the weather is nice, they play catch outside. The games and activities are planned, so that all students can participate, regardless of their disability.

On weekdays, the OEI staff has a half hour devotional time. There is a different topic each day, and on this Monday morning Amanda and Hannah were asked to give the devotion. They began with a few worship songs and shared a little about themselves. They shared their interest in seeing how Operation of Equip India serves young people with disabilities and their desire to serve alongside OEI during their two weeks there. They closed with a couple of Scriptures. Throughout the rest of the day, Amanda and Hannah were given a tour of the Center and shown the different departments and what each does.

Before lunch, I spoke to the students who were close to finishing their training and education at OEI and returning to their home villages. I encouraged them in their future endeavors, emphasizing that they would not encounter the acceptance or wheelchair accessibility in their villages, as they had at OEI. My sharing brought many students to tears, especially the girls, as many of them did not want to return to their village. It was heartbreaking to see them so distraught over having to return to their homes. OEI had become their home, a place where they were loved, accepted and respected for who they were as a person.

The time arrived for the rest of our team to join us in Hubli. Karen and the OEI team picked up Jon, Vicky, and George from the train station. It was a very hot day, and I thought Jon was being a "good sport" traveling on the trains in India, especially when temperatures were 100 degrees Fahrenheit or more. Unfortunately, George had gotten sick on the train, possibly from the food eaten on the train ride, and Jon seemed to be a bit dehydrated. As soon as they returned to the Center, their room having been made ready, George lay down and was given cold water and a cool towel to reduce his temperature.

The colorful welcome

Once George settled, we made certain he was as comfortable as possible. Vicky also looked very tired, but her main concern was Jon and George. While this was transpiring, a few of the OEI staff were busy setting up the table for lunch. Everyone was refreshed after resting and cooling down, and were all able to enjoy a delicious hot meal.

The next item on our agenda was the formal welcome of guests. OEI has a tradition that I call the "Colorful Welcome." The guests of honor are seated at the head of the table and are welcomed with colored water splashed on them. Guests take off any watches and other articles of jewelry that they did not want to get wet. Each guest quietly braced himself/herself, as the hosts brought a bucket of water and poured colored powder into each one. They asked a few people what color they wanted in the bucket, but after several colors are mixed together, the liquid becomes very murky and colors are undistinguishable. They then begin to toss the water from one bucket to another and everyone cringes, and while pausing, they add more colored powder. They swish the water back and forth between the two buckets one more time, and then the content of one bucket is tossed at the apprehensive guests. But instead of colored water, small yellow flowers rained down upon them. During the mixing, someone had stealthily switched the buckets. Each guest felt foolish for his/her anxiety, and Jon was even disappointed that he did not get drenched with the murky water, so I dipped my fingers into the pack of colored powder and wiped his cheek. This act began a series of color swipes across everyone in the great hall. Lastly, they performed an ancient tradition of laying fresh flower garlands around the guest's necks. Then we were served tea and sweets.

Later that evening, we spent time with the students again, providing time for Jon, Vicky, and George to get acquainted with the students. We dined together and chatted about the students' interests and learned what majors or vocational training programs they were pursuing. This conversation provided everyone on our team an opportunity to familiarize themselves with the students' experiences as persons with disabilities in their local community, as well as on OEI's campus. Several of the female students were in the vocational training program and also attending classes in spoken English, some were in the teacher education program, and a few were working toward their junior college diploma. Some male students were completing undergraduate and graduate college/university degrees in majors such as social work, teaching, computer science or engineering. All indicated an interest in socializing, building friendships, reading, computers, and sports, especially the game of cricket.

College and Career Day

At the next morning staff devotional time, Jon shared his story on how he became disabled. The remainder of the day was devoted to helping the students with their career plans and providing advice on building careers. OEI invited both their former and current students, so there were approximately 100 college and career-age people, plus others with whom OEI had built relationships, all with disabilities.

I was asked to speak at the first session of the program and had decided it should be more of a discussion, so I questioned the students as to how they were preparing themselves for getting a job and shared some tips on job preparation for someone with disabilities. We discussed the importance of an updated resume and preparation for an interview. For example, most of these students come from low income families and do not have many clothes. Important to their preparation was to have one set of clothing, preferably a neutral color, washed and ironed, so it would be always ready for an interview. Also critical was arriving at the interview 30 minutes early, even if they had to wait. The importance of follow-up with companies and organizations was also discussed, and it was suggested that if they had not heard from the potential employer, to contact him/her to learn what decision had been made. I encouraged them to apply at many different places, not just to one job at a time, explaining to them that applying for a job was a full-time job in itself. After lunch Jon showed his video, "More than Walking" for the college and career age group, encouraging them to think beyond their disability. Later on, Vicky gave a motivational talk, telling the students not to allow their disability to discourage them from realizing their dream, but in fact, their disability should be a motivation.

The other members of our team, who were not teaching or training the young people, were assigned elsewhere. Hannah worked with the handicraft department, learning what they do and to offer her talents in drawing designs for bags and clothing. She designed a few handicrafts, choosing complementary colors for it. I was counseling the vocational training students, so Amanda joined me, as her major is in counseling and she wanted to watch how I communicated with the people. Normally, I counsel with the help of an interpreter. However, the first few students spoke my first language, Hindi. Since Amanda could not understand us, I shared a summary of what we discussed after each session. At the end of the day, we all came together, had tea and snacks with our 100 guests, we could not take a big group picture but took a few photos, and said our "goodbyes."

Jon, Vicky and George were departing after dinner, so Karen, accompanied by the OEI team, gave them a hardy send off at the train station. The next

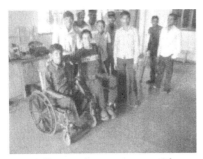

morning Amanda and I, with some of the OEI staff, would be departing for Disability Ministry Trainings in Davengere and Chitradurga. The details of our trip and the training there are in a later chapter.

College and career group with disabilities

After being gone for almost a week, Amanda and I returned to Hubli and arrived after midnight. We were very tired, so we immediately went to bed. However, a few hours later Amanda woke up feverish and vomiting. I had hoped her temperature would go down on its own, but by late that afternoon, her temperature had risen. This was

my first experience having anyone from my team so sick. There was no ice available to cool her, and the only water available was the drinking water in the refrigerator, and even that was lukewarm, due to a power outage. I stayed by Amanda's side, continually praying and replacing cold compresses, while Hannah kept changing the water bowl for the compresses. By nightfall, her temperature finally started going down. The following morning, Amanda was able to keep some food in her stomach, but she still had a temperature, so Cindy took her to the doctor. Antibiotics were administered, and her temperature returned to normal. As a team leader, I definitely felt moments of concern, but thanks to God, He answered our prayers and took care of Amanda.

The next three days were reserved for Karen to provide training for the OEI staff. She focused on early intervention, learning disabilities, postural alignment, and lifting and carrying strategies. She reviewed a full scope of currently defined learning disabilities. The staff learned adaptations to posture and how to prevent injuries. Early intervention was also stressed, as this is the primary factor impacting outcome. Details in the Appendix.

Training for volunteers working with people with HIV/AIDS

I did bereavement training for the new staff and volunteers working with families impacted by HIV/AIDS. All the trainees were very enthusiastic and involved in the discussion, especially those who had lost a family member and had gone through the grieving process. For some, the topic was a vivid reminder that they were still grieving the loss. For many, the session emphasized the need to heal from their own hurt, before they could help others who were recently diagnosed with HIV/AIDs or had lost a family member to HIV/AIDs.

On the day before our departure from Hubli, Hannah and Amanda led the staff in worship songs during morning devotions. After the devotional time, while the staff went to work, we were given the opportunity to do last minute shopping at OEI's handicraft department, with all the wonderful products. There were bags, purses, wallets, book marks, jewelry pouches, table runners, and cushion covers with elaborate embroidery work. We were faced with the dilemma of having more items to pack in our already full luggage, but one of the enjoyable parts of traveling is the many beautiful things brought home for yourself and as gifts for others. It was also exciting to buy things that had been made by our new friends with disabilities at OEI.

The skills they acquired through the vocational training program would help provide for themselves and their families, and we could now encourage them through the purchase of their beautiful handiwork.

In the evening, we were invited for dinner at Tommy and Cindy's home. Tommy works with the International Team division and Cindy is a physical therapist. I was apprehensive about my ability to visit their first floor apartment, as India's first floor is the second floor in the United States. However, since they so very much wanted us to join them for dinner in their home, we finally agreed to come. To reach their home, there was a narrow staircase with a tight turn. In order to gain access to the "first floor" the outer rims of my wheelchair had to be removed so that my wheelchair would fit through the narrow staircase and squeeze around the tight turn of the stairwell. There was only enough room for one person in front of the wheelchair and one behind it. Each of the steps was narrower in depth and higher than

Decked out for a party

an average step. This made maneuvering each step very difficult for the person behind me, and I became increasingly concerned. Never before had I been this anxious for someone who was carrying me up a staircase. Once we reached the top of the staircase, we were on the balcony of their apartment. Everything else in their home was accessible for my wheelchair. They had prepared a lovely dinner of soup, noodles, and other traditional Indian food. We enjoyed the delicious food, and we shared with them our experiences at OEI. We all used this time to debrief, discussing our time and work with them. Tommy thanked us and complimented us for all our services and for being so very helpful. He asked when our next trip to Hubli would be and how else we could be involved with OEI.

Our team had one last opportunity to shop in Hubli, so Karen, Amanda, and Hannah went. It was a hot day. When they returned, Karen was not feeling very well, as she had spent so much time in the hot sun. She needed to lie down and rest, so she missed the OEI farewell ceremony prior to our leaving for the airport. Different staff members expressed words of appreciation for our service at OEI. They showed a DVD of the pictures they had taken during our time there. Then we had the opportunity to speak, so Amanda and Hannah said a few things and I followed with some words of appreciation for their hospitality and how much we enjoyed working with them. We all were sad to leave. After a closing prayer, we had tea and snacks, and then we headed to the airport for our flight to New Delhi. We had a few final days in New Delhi before leaving to flying back to the United States.

During our time in Hubli with OEI, I had provided training with their team to four other cities in the state of Karnataka. Those cities and the details of our work there are included in the next chapters.

6

Mundgod

Operation Equip India had planned a two day program for their leadership, calling it "Leaders Meet." The meeting was held in Mundgod, a small town two-hour's drive from Hubli. Mundgod is known for being the "mini Tibet" in India. The 2001 census reported Mundgod's population to be 16,171, with a literacy rate of 67%. Part of this population includes Tibetan refugees. In the early 1960s, after years of Chinese invasions into the country of Tibet, the Central Tibetan Administration petitioned the Indian government to assist the persecuted Tibetans, by setting up refugee camps in India for them. The Indian government agreed and allotted them several areas, including 4,000 acres in the forest lands of Mundgod. This is the largest community of Tibetan refugees. In 1966 nearly 15,000 refugees called Mundgod their home. There are now 20,000 refugees living in Mundgod, of which 7,000 are monks. The large settlement was then divided into smaller camps or sub-settlements. The refugees were initially provided tents, bamboo huts, and free dry rations.

The Dalai Lama visited Mundgod in 1995 and in 2008 for the inauguration of the new Drepung monastery, a replica of the 500 year old monastery destroyed by the Chinese in 1959. There are a total of seven monasteries devoted to the Mahayana-Buddhist theological education and the pursuit of monastic lifestyle. Many of the people are farmers, producing such agricultural products as rice, corn, and cotton. Other options include crafts, such as woolen products and beautiful carpets.

Nearby is the Attiveri Bird Sanctuary, which is surrounded by a ravine and deciduous forests. This sanctuary is home to the Indian shag, cattle egret, little cormorant, spoonbill, pied kingfisher, white ibis, white-breasted kingfisher, Indian Grey Hornbill and common swallow. Mundgod's nearest railroad station and airport is in Hubli which is 50 km (31 miles) away. In the settlement, there are restaurants and shops to purchase Tibetan gifts and crafts.

One of OEI's contacts operated an orphanage in Mundgod, in a building that had been built two years prior to our visit. Part of the building is used for the orphanage, while the other half is used as a conference center for different organizations within driving distance. These organizations rent the conference center for a short period of time to conduct conferences and retreats, and the money received is used for the orphanage and the upkeep of the building. The orphanage cares for children of toddler age through high school. A few of these children have disabilities, as well. It was encouraging to realize that children with disabilities were welcomed and included, even though the main focus of the orphanage was not directed toward those children.

The purpose of the OEI Leadership meeting was to discuss what had been achieved during the past two years, in accordance with their three-year plan. If the goals had not been met, the barriers to meeting those goals would need to be addressed and new strategies would have to be developed.

Karen and I had been invited to participate in the meeting to observe and because we were acquainted with the organization's vision over the past several years. The leadership valued us, as a third party observer, to offer our insight and give our objective perspective of the presentations by the directors of each department and the discussions that followed. It was very interesting and encouraging to hear the details and the in-depth effort of each department in making a difference in the lives of the people with disabilities. The meeting also gave each department the opportunity to practice presenting their reports prior to showing the final draft to the board. Training and counseling were also provided to the staff to correct and revise their reports, in order to fulfill the requirements of the board and the state law.

We arrived in Mundgod at nine in the morning and were directed to our rooms to relax and unpack. Karen and I shared a room, and the other ladies shared the adjacent room. All the men were assigned rooms in a different section. It is customary in gatherings like this for the men and women to be in separate locations. Even couples are separated, because the focus of the event is not about couples being together. It is also more sensitive to the singles and those who had come without their spouse.

After unpacking, we had breakfast in our room. Karen and I ate all our meals in our room, because the dining room was not wheelchair accessible. In order for me to travel to the dining hall, I would have had to be carried in my wheelchair through a narrow door and down five steep steps. This would have been dangerous for both me and those carrying me. Then, my wheelchair would have to be pushed across a rocky yard and up five or six steeper and narrower steps into the dining hall. So to avoid that hassle and the dangers for everyone involved, the decision was made that all our meals would be served in our room.

After breakfast, we gathered for a meeting in a large hall, where everyone sat on the bare floor. It began with a brief time of devotion and prayer, followed by the presentations of each department, ending with a discussion about the information just presented. Lastly, there was a time for questions, which I was looking forward to, as there were several things that were unclear to me.

The director of the orphanage had made wonderful arrangements for each meal. Tea and snacks were served between meals in the conference hall. Fortunately, whenever power was lost, the orphanage had a generator for part of the building, which provided the needed electricity. Consequently, everyone was able to use his/her computer and give power points presentation with uninterrupted electricity for the majority of the time.

Work of OEI Departments

The Friends Department, which provides spiritual support and counseling to individuals with disabilities and their families, gave the first presentation. This department provides a support system for the person with the disability and family counseling, that encourages the family members to provide quality care. The department also arranges camps and rallies for young people with disabilities, creating hope for the individual and a vision for the community. The department maintains close contact with both current and former clients. On a weekly basis, postcards are sent in reply to letters received, as well as to check how previous clients are doing. They often visit former students and invite some to come to the Center to discuss their problems and needs. The Friends Department also provides a correspondence school for Bible Study for those who are interested

The Socio-Economic and Educational Development (SEED) department focuses on a "person centered approach" to develop skills and nurture abilities to help each individual reach his/her full potential. The team includes ten staff members, plus the director, who are involved in Institution Based Rehabilitation (IBR) activities. Team activities include vocational training, education, tutoring, computer training, tricycle manufacturing and distribution, job placements and much more. They also provide counseling for clients, because for many, this is the first time that many are living in a dormitory or are in an educational environment.

The International Relations and Donor Communications Department (IDRC) plans and arranges training for the international teams who come to India. This department works to build relationships and communication with international contacts. They are also responsible for raising financial support for students who are in the OEI vocational training program or pursuing higher education. They are responsible for accommodating visiting teams coming to serve in various ways, including the Wheels for the World team, who come every year to distribute wheelchairs to clients and others in need of mobility devices. Three international teams served in 2010: My team, Wheels for the World, and a construction team.

The Community Based Rehabilitation (CBR) Department travels from village to village, advocating for people with disabilities to maximize their talents and abilities, to present them with the opportunities that OEI offers, and to demonstrate how they can lead independent lives in their communities. Members of this department walk through the villages to connect with families who have someone with a disability. Upon meeting these families, they evaluate their needs, so that OEI can determine how they can be best served. CBR also establishes training for the families and other villagers, providing instruction on how to practice personal wellness. This instruction includes pregnancy care, normal development education, and ways to stimulate development, among other relevant topics. Since most of these villages do not have an adequate water supply, CBR provides water pumps.

The Physical Medicine and Rehabilitation Department (PMR) seeks to improve the quality of life and reduce the risks of any secondary complications of disability, through assessment physiotherapy and providing mobility aids and Orthotic appliances (Calipers, Braces, and Splints), all from a professional medical approach. Clients call the director, who is a physical therapist, "Doctor." She does the initial evaluation, which determines whether or not the client could benefit from physical therapy. Once approved for the program, the "Doctor" teaches the individuals and their families how to perform the various therapy exercises. She also provides therapy for outpatients and students who are living in the dorm, depending on their specific situation. In some cases, the initial evaluation may also determine whether or not corrective surgery may benefit the individual, and if it is determined that it would, an appointment with the orthopedic surgeon for a second evaluation is made. If an individual goes through corrective surgery, the therapist provides the follow-up therapy. During this process, often clients stay in the dorm, so their rehabilitation progress can be observed.

In a previous trip during the summer of 2008, Karen, Judy, an occupational therapist, and I stayed at OEI. There were two students, male and female, who recently had had corrective surgery and were still in their casts. During our visit, the two students had their casts removed, and were subsequently fitted for braces which would arrive several weeks later. When I returned six months later, I learned that the girl had finished her vocational training and had returned to her village. I was also told that she had physical therapy as well, and was now starting to walk with her braces. The male student was still at the dorm continuing his college education. He also had continued therapy and was able to walk with braces. He seemed very happy with his new found independence. Many of the OEI clients arrive without the ability to walk or stand, but return home with newly acquired mobility, due to the treatment received at PMR. To see an individual begin to walk for the first time is always exciting for the OEI staff and family members!

Previously, Cindy only met with clients at the OEI clinic for the initial evaluation. However, currently she visits the villages to see clients. She also visits medical clinics for initial evaluations, set up by the churches in the district where OEI hosts its Disability Ministry Seminars. Karen and I were very surprised to witness the amount of work Cindy and others do through the PMR department. I thought that the PMR department needed at least one more full time physical therapist, but I did not mention that or ask about its possibility, as hiring additional staff was not being discussed at that time.

Through the Vocational Training (VT) Department, ladies are trained by the "Equip India's Handicraft Department" (EIH) to embroider and stitch bags, clothes, and other clothing products. Once their vocational training is completed, they have the option to work for EIH from their homes. They pick up the material from EIH, complete the project at home and then return the finished product. It is then sold to pay the salary of the home worker. It is amazing that their salary can provide for the family's basic needs and assist families with disability-related expenses. Some families were even able to build small living quarters with an attached accessible bathroom.

Each year, more home workers are trained, increasing production. We discussed ways to increase net sales as the number of workers increased to cover the worker's salaries. I recommended that someone focus his/her time to market the products. There is a small shop in a mall in New York City which sells their handicrafts. Sales increase around Christmas time, but sales needed to significantly grow in the upcoming year. We also discussed setting up handicraft displays at the entrance to the OEI Center and other NGOs, to help sell the merchandise. Karen noted that the production goal for the following year bore **no** relationship to the number of workers available, so it did not reflect the current production capacity of the workers. She added that the plan did not include a plan to maximize the workers efforts to achieve OEI's production goal.

The Spiritual Enrichment Program (SEP) provides disability ministry seminars to church groups to begin reaching out to people affected by disabilities, leprosy, and HIV/AIDs. OEI had divided the state into North, Central, and South in which to present these seminars. We had completed the Northern Karnataka seminar in 2008-2009. The group was currently working with the central part of the state. The current director was new and still in the process of learning, so he was hesitant to teach any of the sessions if the regular trainers were unable to be at these seminars. However, he is a very capable person and we were certain that as he learns more, he will continue to improve, and consequently, the program will improve and advance. After the seminars, I encouraged him for the future. It was a pleasure to be able to speak with those pastors and churches who were planning disability ministry seminars. The director connects with ministry leaders by phone, email, letters, and he meets with the church leadership in person, always traveling on his motorcycle.

The Finance and Administration department raises funds for OEI special projects. As an example, it arranges provisions for the families affected by

HIV/AIDS to supplement the existing government programs. The director also builds relationships with churches, individuals and other organizations to raise money for OEI's many projects. The department has raised funds well beyond OEI's expectations.

Lastly, the Nirikshe Department serves the community of individuals and families impacted by HIV/AIDS. This department provides the needed resources for children with HIV/AIDS and the children with parents who have HIV/AIDS to remain in school. Sometimes schools choose not to register these students, or the parents of other students do not want them around their children, due to the associated stigma and the belief that it is not worth investing time in what may be a fatal disease. Nirikshe advocates for the families affected by HIV/AIDS and provides support to women with this disease and for women who have lost their husbands and/or children to the disease. Additionally, they assist children who have lost one or both parents to the disease.

In either scenario, the woman is blamed by the family of her husband, and occasionally, by her own family as well. If the husband dies with HIV/AIDS, his wife is blamed for it and often kicked out of the home. Normally, husbands bring in the disease, and then pass it on to their wives and/or children. Women need long-term counseling, assistance with acquiring medication, and applying to the government program that pays for the medication, all of which is provided by Nirikshe. Nirikshe also provides them with dry groceries and helps send their children to school. I provided training on bereavement for this department, so the staff and the volunteers can use what they have learned to provide counseling to those grieving due to a family member's diagnosis of HIV/AIDS or to those who have lost a family member to this terrible disease.

Staff from each department had many responsibilities, and as I met with the volunteers, the sense was that it would be beneficial to add an additional volunteer, so the current overworked staff and volunteers would not experience "burn out." This provision would also provide them additional time to provide better care to more clients. Karen and I observed that most departments were stressed due to high departmental expectations and overload of work. This frustrated the staff, and consequently, negatively impacted their outcomes.

At the end of the sessions, the director of OEI, Elish Kanthi, shared about leadership. The content included topics about what a role model looks like, what denotes good leadership skills, and how to lead and support those being led. Finally, it was emphasized that a leader should acknowledge the others who are a critical part of the team. Following the teaching, Mr. Kanthi complimented each department head and offered suggestions on how they encourage one another through their strengths. Karen and I thought he had done a marvelous job by helping and encouraging those in attendance. This was the end of our time at the Leaders Meet. Then we headed back to Hubli.

Disability Ministry Training
in 3 Districts by OEI

hrough the Spiritual Enrichment Program (SEP), OEI trains churches in many districts in the north, south, and central parts of the state of Karnataka. Each district has five Taluks (sub-districts), and one or two churches in each of these districts were identified as being leaders and recruiting others for leadership from sub-district churches. I had traveled with OEI's training team to three different districts (cities) in the state of Karnataka to provide Disability Ministry training. Those cities (Sagar, Davengere and Chitradurga)- and the details of our work there are included in this chapter.

The church leadership from the above-mentioned cities invited the churches from their five Taluks. In each district, 95% of the attendees were men. We conducted the first training in Sagar, consisting of an introduction to OEI, understanding disability, the stigma related to disability, and HIV/ AIDS awareness. I concluded with the teaching on "God's Heart for the Disabled."

Sagar

Karen and I, with the OEI Training team, traveled five hours to Central Karnataka. We left early in the morning, stopping only briefly for food.

Traveling by van on the rough roads made it a rather torturous journey. Instead of five hours, however, it took us seven hours due to the poor road conditions and heavy traffic.

The city of Sagar was named for a nearby lake, and the city was built by *Sadashiva Sagar*, a ruler of the Kelardi Dynasty. The city is surrounded by a number of bodies of water and the Varada River, which provides the water needs of the people in the area. The economy is sustained by the major cash crop of betel nut, which helps support the growing population of fifty thousand. Gudigars is a common form of trade. It involves the making of a certain form of sandalwood and ivory carvings that has been a family enterprise for generations.

An interesting feature in the city is a common wall which is shared by a Ganapathi Temple and a local Muslim Mosque. It is believed to have its roots in the attack from the kings, Hyder Ali (Muslim ruler in the 18th century) and Tippu Sultan (Hindu king), on the kingdom of Keladi. However, no one knows for certain why the wall supports two extremely different religious buildings. The closest tourist destination to Sagar is Honnemardu Reservoir, a beautiful lake created by a dam in 1965. The nearest airport is 316 kilometers away at Bangalore. Sagar is also one of only two places in the world, Zululand in South Africa being the other, where the people have a very rare skeletal disorder called Handigodu Syndrome, which causes joint swelling, dwarfism, deformation of limbs, and early death in their late 20s.

We arrived in Sagar, but had no hotel reservation. The local team didn't think it would be a problem to get a room at any hotel, so they chose not to book a room for us ahead of time. However, we drove from hotel to hotel searching for a room that was wheelchair accessible. One of the recommended hotels claimed to have an accessible room, but it required climbing forty very steep steps to reach it. Everyone was tired from traveling in the ninety degree heat and high humidity, so the men thought that, if the room suited us, they were willing to carry me. None of us were comfortable with the situation, as Karen and Cindy, being physical therapists, were concerned someone might hurt his/her back or lose his/her balance while carrying me up the stairs. However, the men insisted, so Cindy measured the bathroom door to make certain the effort was worth it. The door width was narrower than my wheelchair, so with relief, we resumed our search for a suitable hotel room. Finally, after four hours and since it was getting very late, we registered at a hotel, even thought it was not accessible. We reasoned that it was only sixteen steps up to the room rather than forty! We settled into the room, realizing again that the wheelchair would not fit into the bathroom. We tried taking the outer rims of the wheels off, but to no avail. I became very concerned that I would not be able to take a shower after the day of high temperatures and a hot night without air conditioning. I left the situation in the Lord's hand.

The two pastors that had organized the training session visited us at the hotel. We discussed the program and schedule for the following day. The pastors informed us that the city was going to be under curfew, because some in the Muslim community were offended by a book being printed in the city. The book was written by a former Muslim, and the community disagreed with what the author wrote.

The ladies stayed at the hotel, while the men stayed at the pastor's home for the night. Karen and I reviewed the PowerPoint slides for our presentation, prayed together and then went to bed. It was a very hot and humid night. and I had difficulty sleeping due to the lack of air conditioning, and the noise from the street.

Our team was scheduled to arrive at the training site by nine o'clock the following morning to check the PA system and set up our computers. Arriving there would also allow us ample time to pray with the team from Sagar before the guests arrived. After breakfast, the men carried me down the sixteen steps to the main floor and then loaded the van. In spite of the disturbance in the city, we arrived at the site without any delays. By the time the program started all the pastors and others community leaders had arrived. There was great interest in the information we provided, and we were greatly pleased with the insightful questions and comments.

My session was the last one of the day and was designed to challenge the leaders to actively reach out to the people with disabilities in their communities. As I was speaking, I noticed positive reactions on the faces in the audience. I shared the church's response to the community of people with disability in the light of Biblical mandate, stating that the church had not always followed through in serving this community. People in the audience had tears in their eyes and intermittently nodded their heads. I explained to them that many pastors and church leaders, as well as others, had an important role in shaping my life. I asked them if they would be willing to take a more active role in shaping the lives of those with disability in their community. Many in the audience responded by raising their hands and saying, "Yes," assuring me that they understood and were in agreement with the message.

After the seminar, the two key pastors requested that I remain on the platform. They joined me and invited Karen to join us. Each pastor took

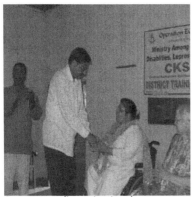

Pastor complimenting in a language we did not understand

a few minutes and talked directly to us, then prayed for us and placed garlands around our necks. During this time, no one interpreted for us, so we were not certain what they were saying. I only understood a few words that were spoken. Later in the van, we asked the OEI team members what had been said during our time on the platform. They shared that the pastors were thanking us for being there, thanking me for sharing my life story, and for teaching the group. Our presentations had inspired them tremendously, encouraging them to involve themselves in disability ministry in the near future.

Davangere

It was time to travel again, this time to Davengere for another Disability Ministry Training session. Amanda accompanied me, while Karen and

Hannah remained in Hubli to work with the OEI staff and students. Amanda and I awoke early to prepare for the day and went to the dining room for tea. The kitchen staff had prepared breakfast for us, but neither of us wanted to eat so early in the morning. Begrudgingly, we both had tea and a piece of toast, and then boarded the van. Once our driver secured my wheelchair, we drove into the city to pick up other team members and equipment. Finally, we were on our way to Davangere.

Davengere is in the state of Karnataka and functions as the headquarters for the administration of the Davengere district, more like the capital of the district. It is located approximately 265 kilometers (about 165 miles) from the state capital of Bangalore. Davengere is also under the taluk, which includes the cities of Davangere, Harihar, Jagalur, Honnali, Channagiri, and Harpanhalli. In 2001, the census indicated that Davengere had a population of 363,780 people with a literacy rate of 69%, a rate higher than the overall literacy rate of India (59.5%). Since 2001, the population has exploded to 1,478,425. The primary language spoken is Kannada, but Hindi and English are also spoken because of the large student population in the city.

Davangere, also called the Manchester of Karnataka due to the concentration of textile mills, is known for being the major trading center of Karnataka as the town was given to Apoji Ram under the reign of Sultan Haider Ali. It was later turned into a cotton mill village. The status of being a merchant city, and the increased need for cotton lifted the citizens of Davangere to a higher income level, and consequently, they began donating to social programs for the poor and for the building of a local hospital. Davangere is also an educational center with three major engineering colleges, two dental colleges, two medical colleges, a number of management schools and colleges, an art college, and a fashion design college. There are significant educational efforts emerging in the district to assist those with disabilities. Samveda is a training school which teaches people with learning disabilities. They not only want to reach out to those with disabilities, but they also reach out to parents, teachers, and doctors who are working with the disabled.

After a couple hours of driving, we stopped for tea and breakfast at a small café. We ordered Idli, a rice puff patty and a local lentil and vegetable broth dip. Since the majority of the roads are rough and traffic is dense, it's helpful to stop every two to three hours, especially for the driver's sake. The journey was slow because of the many trucks along our path. At one point, the traffic came to a complete stop, and the truckers were so bored that they were hanging out of their windows and looking into our van, staring at both Amanda and me. My permed hair had become large and bushy because of the wind, humidity, and dirt. That, combined with the lightest skinned western girl they had ever seen and speaking with a thick American accent, made for an interesting trip, to say the very least! Overall, the drive was pleasant and Amanda thoroughly enjoyed taking pictures along our route. One OEI staff member started a conversation with Amanda, but she struggled in her understanding of what he was saying due to his thick Indian accent, and he struggled greatly with her American accent. They were both speaking English, but neither one was able to understand a word the other was saying, so I had to interpret everything. It was very interesting to translate English to English.

Stopping for lunch, we found a nice, wheelchair accessible, restaurant that from outward appearances did not appear to be a restaurant at all. The entrance had an easy ramp and the interior was spacious and clean. The bathroom door was even wide enough for my chair to enter, with a clean, western style toilet. Their menu was easy to understand and had entrees that westerners would appreciate, especially if they did not enjoy spicy Indian food. My wheelchair and I were entertainment for the other diners. It gave them something to stare at, whisper, and wonder about. Every once in awhile, I had fun staring back at them and smiling, at which point, not knowing what to do, they avoided eye contact. After lunch, we finished our journey to Davengere and arrived at the hotel around dinner time. Cindy, Amanda, and I checked into a room together on the first floor (which really is the second floor), while the men checked into their shared room. We were all tired from the heat and travel, so the men carried me up the stairs to my room and then went to their room to relax.

Later, the men brought us dinner, but the only thing I wanted was a cold soda. However, even a cold beverage would quickly turn warm after five minutes in our hands. It was hard to sleep in a 37 degrees Celsius (100 degrees Fahrenheit) room with only a fan to cool us. The fan was only circulating warm air, but at least we were not sleeping in our own sweat. I know I slept better in the latter half of the night, when the temperature finally dropped into the 80's (F°) degrees.

Amanda eating granola bar with a spoon

The next morning, Cindy and Amanda helped me get into the bathroom, requiring Cindy tilting the wheelchair back on two wheels to rest the front wheels on the ten inch high step, and then Amanda pulling my wheelchair up from the front. Amanda then pulled me into the bathroom, while Cindy pushed from the back and lifted the back wheels. It was an ordeal. Once inside the bathroom, I was able to maneuver my chair easily, because there was enough space. Unfortunately, there was no shower bench, so I covered my chair with a sheet of plastic in order to use the shower. When I finished, Amanda and Cindy helped me out of the bathroom, reversing the process. I hope these details draw a clear picture of what a burden it is for a wheelchair user to do daily activities that others do easily and take for granted. One can never predict what obstacles may lay ahead, so in my travels, I always need to be forward thinking and creative in order to manage in various non-accessible environments. While I was finishing preparing for the day, the men had brought our breakfast to the room, as the hotel did not have a restaurant. Men from our team had to go out to a small café to buy breakfast, since the clientele at the café was predominately men and it was not socially appropriate for women to be there. Additionally, it was inaccessible for my wheelchair. Amanda ate her granola bar, which was an interesting sight, as it had melted and she had to eat it with a spoon, using the wrapper as her plate and carefully scooping each bite.

The training site was at a local church with an attached parsonage, not far from our hotel. The pastor requested that we park the van as close to the building as possible, so we could quickly be escorted out of the van, directly into the church. They were extra cautious because this particular community was not friendly to westerners and adverse to western cultural influences. The relatively new church building was large and could easily seat 500 people. One hundred chairs had been set up in rows near the front of the church, while the back was filled with tables and stacks of chairs along the back wall, which were reserved for lunch and beverages.

Pastor John, who was the primary organizer for this event, sat next to me, prior to the seminar, and he shared with me how timely my visit was. His sister, a polio survivor, had been a wheelchair user and had her own NGO

People present at the training

in a neighboring city devoted to helping persons with disabilities there. She had died a few years earlier, and her NGO closed its door, because the family did not have the time or the ability to run it. Pastor John had the desire to revive the ministry, and when he heard about my visit to India through OEI, he was very encouraged. I was delighted to encourage him further and hoped to be instrumental in helping him restart the NGO.

Since I was traveling from the United States, my name was not advertised as one of the trainers. Therefore the attendees were not expecting me to be there. The only one who had known I was coming was Pastor John. Another pastor, Sunil, who did not know I was coming, sat next to me and told me what an encouragement it was to have me at a disability event. It did not occur to him that I would be speaking later, which was, perhaps, because I was a woman or disabled. It was interesting to witness the surprise on his face when my teaching session began. The director of CKSEP introduced the organization (OEI), Cindy taught the session "understanding disability" and the impact of disability on individual and his/her family, Arnold reviewed the stigma associated with disability, he also talked about the holistic approach to

Joy teaching at the last session in Davengere

help the disability community, Peter spoke about HIV/AIDS. Lastly, I spoke on God's Heart for the Disabled.

People were very attentive through all the sessions, and when given the opportunity to ask questions, they were excited to interact with the staff. Even after the conclusion, people continued coming up, asking questions regarding how they could start a ministry in their church. At the debriefing afterwards, Pastor John was very encouraged by the number of participants who had indicated an interest in starting disability ministry in their churches.

Pastor Sunil invited us to his house for a cup of coffee, so we all helped load the van and drove to his house. His wife, daughter, son, and elderly mother were waiting for us. We had a very nice visit and were served a delicious snack, freshly made out of cauliflower, with coffee and tea. It was a very comfortable apartment, with a living room and a dining room divided by a curtain. A small window in the living room was cracked, and the pastor noticed that I was scrutinizing it. He explained that his neighborhood was a very anti-Christian community, and it was very common for Christians to find their property damaged. Either people throw stones, or bang on the windows and doors with hockey sticks or bats.

Before leaving, the pastor's mother shared something with us which I was not able to understand. The pastor and his wife seemed hesitant to translate, but then told us what his mother had said. "I have only two children, this son who is a pastor and another son who, two years ago, went out of the house and never came back. His wife and child have been living with his wife's parents.

Pray that my son would return." Pastor Eric added, "We do not even know if he is still alive, but it is hard for our mother to accept that my brother may have been killed or committed suicide." It was a really heartbreaking story. I asked one of the OEI team members to pray in the language most similar to the pastor's mother' first language, so that she would understand the prayer.

The next day, we were scheduled to go to Pastor John's house to discuss how to start a Disability Ministry in their church. We enjoyed a free morning, and after brunch, we went out shopping. After shopping, we returned to wait for Pastor John's phone call. When he did call to set up a time to meet, we decided that I would not accompany them, so the men would not have to carry me down and up the staircase again. Amanda and I stayed in the room, which was hotter than it was the outside. The following morning, we drove two hours to the next district, Chitradurga, for our final Disability Ministry Training.

Chitradurga

Chitradurga is a two to three hour drive from Davangere. The city is smaller and in a more remote area, especially with regard to the location of our destination church. There were no hotels in Chitradurga, so we decided to stay one more night in Davengere and leave for Chitradurga early in the morning on the day of the seminar. The roads were rough, so it took us longer than we expected to reach our destination.

Chitradurga is the namesake of a third century BCE castle called Chitradurga. It is also known for its large boulders that give it the appearance of a fortress. Among the many hills are mineral deposits and gold and copper mine operations, which provide many local jobs. The hills also contain the Chandravalli caves, where tourists can view old wall paintings, living spaces, bathtubs, places of worship and a treasury. The British name for the area was Chitaldroog. The landscape of the city is picturesque with the valleys and rocks of different shapes scattered throughout the region.

The Chitradurga district consists of the following taluks: Chitradurga,

Hiriyur, Hosadurga, Holalkere, Challakere, and Molakalmuru. According to 2001 statistics, the population was 1,517,896. The vast majority of the population speaks Kannada, but in the areas bordering Andhra Pradesh, some speak Telugu.

Once we arrived in Chitradurga, one of the local pastors met us on his motorcycle and led us to the church. The church was built with bamboo, banana and palm leaves. Since the building had no concrete walls or ceiling heated by the sun, it was amazingly cooler than any other place we had been. There was a little breeze coming through the small cracks in the walls and several ceiling fans, which helped circulate the inside air. The church was large enough to seat 200 people, and the pastor had a small living space attached to the church in the rear of the structure.

Once we arrived at the church, we met with Pastor Sam, who had organized the seminar. Pastor Sam had invited many other pastors and church leaders from the area, and from the 5 sub-districts, out of which 40 people were able to attend. The director of the training program introduced OEI team members, shared briefly about OEI and the stated goals of the seminar. At the end of his introduction, everyone had the opportunity to ask questions and make comments. Following are some examples of the question and comments:

$ *How do we reach the disabled?*

$ *Many are shut-ins.*

$ *Some families may not even want help because they believe disability in their family is a curse and because of their bad karma.*

$ *Some communities are anti-Christian, so they would not want us to enter their communities or home.*

$ *Some have completely given up hope regarding their disabled family member so may not be ready to listen to anything.*

$ *We do not have transportation to take them to any disability program, if they want to come.*

People had many questions and expressed their fears and concerns about starting disability ministries in their churches. This dialogue transpired in the local Kanada language, which I do not speak. However, I had been in the state of Karnataka every year for the past 5 years, so I was able to understand much of their conversation. I realized that the people's concerns and fears were preventing them from looking at the disability ministry from a positive perspective.

Raising my hand to get everyone's attention, I was given the floor, and I spoke directly to the group. I noted that everyone seemed to be looking at only the problems and the risks involved, but my point was that nothing worthwhile is without risks. I added that all of the pastors, when they started their ministry in their areas, knew there would be risks and -challenges. As their churches grew, different departments and programs were added and/or expanded, and with any change comes the potential for failure, vulnerability and problems. I concluded by recommending that we begin the sessions and remember that our ultimate problem solver is Christ Himself. I encouraged us all to focus on the Problem Solver and not on the problems. I added that at the end of each session, as well as at the end of the day, they would have an opportunity to ask questions. I also mentioned that there would be follow-up assistance to help with starting disability ministry. Lastly, I exhorted them to remember that these families and individuals have been hurting for years, and no one has ever shown concern for either the one who is disabled or their families. These comments seemed to encourage the listeners, and they began to respond more optimistically.

Each session was very informative, and at about midway, we took a lunch break. Our food was served on plates made from dried leaves, which made a very unique presentation that was conveniently disposable. By the end of the first session, I began feeling ill. I informed Cindy and Amanda that I felt sick to my stomach and needed to use the restroom. As we were exiting, Cindy mentioned to the pastor's wife about our situation, and she ushered us to the back of the house. She provided a bucket, assuring us that she would keep watch while we improvised. It is amazing how we can "make do" when nothing else is available. I was sick, did not have privacy, and the time for my session was getting closer. This was far from ideal, but my team helped me through it.

Finally, the three of us walked back into the church. Thankfully, the gentleman teaching before me was just concluding his session. I was not certain how I would be able to teach after the whole ordeal I had just endured. However, saying a brief prayer in my heart, asking God to help me do well, I

Joy teaching in the last session at Chitradurga

started teaching. I challenged the group to start a disability ministry in their church, and asked who would be interested in starting this kind of outreach? Most of the church leaders raised their hands. I concluded by encouraging Pastor Sam that his church is fairly accessible, then asking what would be the first thing he would have to do to get started with the disability ministry. He said, "We would need to build an accessible restroom." This was not the answer I was expecting, but I thought it was a great answer after what I had just experienced.

Later, Cindy and Amanda commented on how powerful the presentation had been, and that no-one would have suspected how sick I was just prior to speaking. The seminar was a success, not because of how well I taught, but on how well we worked as a team and the willingness of the audience to learn. After taking a few group pictures and saying our goodbyes, we loaded the vans and secured my wheelchair. It was a long drive back to Hubli as we already

Some of the people at the seminar   *Our team in front of the church*

had a long day, but the success of the seminar was worth the exhaustion.

Follow-up on Sagar, Davengere, & Chitradurga

Sagar

The disability ministry had a slow beginning, due to the diversity of the people involved, but it has received wonderful resources through local social workers and leaders of the community who had been involved in the beginning stages. There is a diversity of people living in the community in terms of literacy level, socio-economic backgrounds, and languages, the latter because some have moved to Sager from a state that speaks a different first language and there are various dialects within the district. However, the ministry was able to organize a mobility aid distribution camp by partnering with OEI. This effort was a huge success, particularly because politicians, who were invited, showed their appreciation of the initiative by pledging their cooperation. Hopefully, this will open doors for finances and advocacy services.

Davengere

Pastor Jon was greatly inspired by the Disability Ministry Training and has since started an assessment camp through local physical therapists. He has also teamed up with OEI to organize a mobility aid distribution camp for people with disabilities in his community. Pastor John is a great leader for their district and has started a disability ministry in his own church. He is keeping in close communication with OEI, with the hope of extending their help and encouragement to the pastors in his sub-districts to start disability ministries in their churches. **Chitradurga**

OEI followed up with Pastor Sam and the other pastors in the Chitradurga District. They found that the pastors had already started planning the disability ministry in their communities. They planned a medical clinic day in one of the sub-districts, and Cindy and others have become part of this clinic. Cindy conducted evaluations with people to assess what type of physical therapy they would need, as well as determine whether or not they would benefit from a mobility aid. OEI brought mobility aids, including crutches, canes, wheelchairs, and walkers, and they were able to distribute several aids to the community. I was pleased to hear that this district was doing very well in starting their disability ministries.

8

Conclusion

What you have read in this book is the product of just one of many trips that have been made over the last several years, assisting the people with disabilities in India. Everyone faces limitations in the course of a lifetime. However, life is a series of choices, and one can either face the personal challenge directly or allow it to restrict their potential. As a person with a disability, I refuse to allow my disability to be the barrier that determines my future. Certainly, my disabilities have slowed me down at times but it can never stop me.

According to my Christian faith, Jesus Christ came to earth, was persecuted, died on a cross and then rose from the dead. He did this with one purpose in mind, to reconcile all mankind to God. My life has been a miracle, because of the answered prayers of my parents. I should have been dead or forever totally paralyzed, but God had a different plan for me. This Divine plan for my life has brought me full circle, as I now have a passion to encourage and work with people with disabilities and their families both here and abroad.

Hopefully, you have caught a glimpse of how powerful it is to open up doors of opportunity to those who have had limited hope for a future. Just imagine if all of us would be a voice to those in need what a ripple effect it would have. As we serve and support people with disabilities, they then give back to their family, church, friends, and community and so the cycle of hopelessness is broken.

Despair can vanish with just a friendly "hello." Avenues of possibility will flow with expectation as you encourage the individuals with disabilities to look at their abilities. Be the cheerleader and persuade them to pursue further education, vocational training, active job searches, and let them know that they also can "pay it forward" by leading the way by example. Community and church leaders also need to "catch the vision" and become strong advocates for the needs of the disability community.

I would like to challenge you to play your part in the lives of the people with disabilities. You may ask, "Where am I going to find these people?" Let me remind you we are everywhere, within your families, churches, communities, neighborhoods, schools, colleges, universities, your work place, parks, beaches, hospitals, nursing homes, on buses, trains, planes, in each and every district, village, city and province on all five continents. You can't miss us! So, join with me and embrace my vision of *A World Without Barriers.*

Appendices

Preface:

http://www.ucl.ac.uk/lc-ccr/lccstaff/raymond-lang/understanding_disability_in_india.pdf

http://sancd.org/uploads/pdf/disability.pdf

http://www.disabilityworld.org/04-05_03/violence/horrorstory.shtml

http://www.disabled-world.com/news/asia/india/

Background:

Varanasi

http://www.varanasicity.com/history-of-varanasi.html

http://www.asiarooms.com/en/travel-guide/india/varanasi/varanasi-overview/history-of-varanasi.html

http://www.lonelyplanet.com/india/uttar-pradesh/Varanasi

http://www.idiscoverindia.com/Travel_Varanasi/Varanasi_facts_figure.html

http://www.isocarp.net/Data/case_studies/1015.pdf

Appendix A

Varanasi

Summary of Joy's talk on "Four Eternal Truths" from The Holy Bible. (Genesis 22: 1-14 NKJV)

The story chronicles God asking Abraham to sacrifice his only son, Isaac. All of God's promises to Abraham and his future generations depended on his son, Isaac. In obedience to God, Abraham was willing to sacrifice his son, because he fully trusted God in this situation. God honored Abraham's obedience by sparing his son Isaac and fulfilling His original covenant (according to the Bible) with Abraham through Isaac. This covenant was God's promise to Abraham and his future generations. This topic was intended to encourage the attendees to be obedient to God and to allow God to honor their obedience to Him. Details of this topic is found in Appendix C.

Appendix C: New Delhi

Summary of Joy's talk, "But He is Strong"

The subject was intended to remind people that God has a plan and purpose for their life. Even if God does not heal someone from disability or terminal illness, He will bring other forms of healing into his or her life. We are made "perfect in weakness," because He is our strength.

Even if God does not heal someone from disability or terminal illness, He brings many other kinds of healing into his or her life, like emotional healing and contentment. The most beautiful thing about God's plan is that with or without disability, God can use each one of us for His glory by using us as a support and encouragement to others in similar situations. "My Grace is sufficient for you, for My strength is made perfect in weakness" (The Holy Bible: 2 Corinthians 12:9 NKJV). I have personally experienced and am often reminded often of how God's grace is sufficient for me and His strength is made perfect in my weakness. Many times I feel weak, not because I have a disability, but because I am human. Let God use us as His instrument to reach out to people with disabilities in India, serving them and building them up, so they can have the confidence to be self sufficient. This will complete God's purpose for the disabled as well as the able-bodied.

Meeting with church leaders

Summary of Jon's talk

As the story goes, when Job's wife told him to forget about God and die, Job responded by saying, "Shall we indeed accept good from God and not accept adversity?" In all this, Job did not sin with his lips" (The Holy Bible: Job 2:10 NKJV). Job's friends said that if God is mighty and powerful, then He could have protected Job from his pain and suffering, but since God had not, Job did not have to be faithful to Him.

"After Job had prayed for his friends, the LORD made him prosperous again and gave him twice as much as he had before" (The Holy Bible: Job 42:10 NKJV). Job's story about suffering and his continual faithfulness to God is still used to encourage people to this day.

Summary of Vicky's talk

"Jon's accident turned our family upside down. I was expecting something like this, because up to this point, Jon was the only member of our family who had not suffered a great personal trauma," Vicky recalled. In 2002, her husband was diagnosed with two forms of cancer within a period of three weeks time. In another incident, her middle son was hit by a car in 2001 while riding his bicycle, and suffered a severe injury. Since 1998, her eldest son has been in and out of psychiatric hospitals.

"We are often told (in our churches) that if we have faith in God we will have a good life, health, wealth and happiness. Suffering with trust in God is not supposed to be part of that deal," Vicky continued.

"It is the unjust suffering of our Lord and Savior, Jesus, which forms the foundation of our faith;" she said adding this quote from the Bible: "Consider it joy when you face trials of many kinds, because you know that the testing of your faith develops perseverance (The Holy Bible: James 1:2 NIV)." "We too can be perfected through suffering. I guess we needed more perfecting," Vicky quipped.

"So in 2006, when Jon fell off a cliff in India, broke his neck, and survived, we were graciously well-prepared to trust God for even such a serious injury as quadriplegia. Through Jon's injury, we have come to love the people of India, and we feel a new kinship with people around the world who have suffered long-term debilitating injuries.

"God does not always protect us from suffering. But He ALWAYS will use it for good in our lives, if we trust him to do so.

"The morning of his accident his Bible study class had just finished discussing the scripture, Romans 8:28 (from the Holy Bible), when they received the call from the hospital about Jon's accident. Since that day, this scripture has become the family's life-verse:"

"And we KNOW that in ALL things God works for the GOOD of those who love Him, who have been called according to His purpose (The Holy Bible: Romans 8:28 NIV)." "What is our goal in life? An easy and prosperous life

? No," "Everyone who is called by God's name has been called to glorify God (The Holy Bible: Isaiah 43:7 NIV) with his/her life." This means following Christ, which guarantees suffering. We are called to be crucified with Christ so that we no longer live, but Christ lives in us (The Holy Bible: Galatians 2:20). In fact, we are promised that everyone who wants to live a godly life in Christ Jesus will be persecuted." (The Holy Bible: 2 Timothy 3:12 NIV).

"God uses the things which we might see as bad or weak, and uses them for good. It's all about God's glory revealed through our weaknesses, not our strengths." Vicky continued, "We have this treasure [the love and knowledge of God] in jars of clay [which are easily broken], to show that this all-surpassing power is from God and not from us" (2 Corinthians 4:7 NIV).

"In fact, the Apostle Paul, who wrote 2 Corinthians, goes even further to share that when he did not get healed of some physical condition, even though he had prayed successfully for the physical healing of many others, he was comforted when God told him that His grace was sufficient for him." "For my [God's] power is made perfect in weakness!"

The apostle went on to say "Therefore, I will boast all the more gladly about my weaknesses, so that Christ's power may rest on me...for when I am weak, then I am [actually] strong [Because of Christ in him]." (The Holy Bible: 2 Corinthians 12:9-10 NIV).

"God's Kingdom is very upside down. The wise are actually foolish, and the foolish are often truly wise, the strong are actually weak, and the weak are often truly strong. I used to look at other's strengths, and wished I was not so weak, but when Jon was injured, our family began to understand the wonderful gift of accepting our weaknesses. Through our weakness, we have seen many wonderful things. And often when we felt the weakest, that is actually when God used us the most to encourage others in their own weaknesses. So, welcome to our upside-down world, where we can even boast of our weaknesses, and be used for the most good when we are often the most weak! Suffering is only truly terrible when one doesn't allow God's redemptive love and transforming power to be used for good."

Appendix B: Kacchwa

http://www.eha-health.org/eha-in-up/kacchwa.html

http://eha-health.org/about.html

http://www.indianetzone.com/12/kachhwa.htm (Same information is also on Wikipedia)

http://en.wikipedia.org/wiki/Kachhwa

Summary of Joy's talk on the
"Parable of the Great Banquet"

The servant came back and reported this to his master. Then the owner of the house became angry and ordered his servant, "Go out quickly into the streets and alleys of the town and bring in the poor, the crippled, the blind and the lame."

Then the master told his servant, "Go out to the roads and country lanes and make them come in, so that my house will be full" (The Holy Bible: Luke 14:21, 23 NIV).

The scripture is about a parable where the master of the house planned a banquet and invited many guests but at the last moment many of the guests gave reasons and informed the servant they would not be able to attend the banquet. The master told the servant to invite a new set of guests and there was still space for more. So the master sent his servant out again saying compel more of them to come to the banquet.

In this scripture, my house refers to God's house which is the church. To be filled with not only non-disabled people, but disabled people as well. This Biblical parable shows the integral place people with disabilities have in the church.

Application of the Parable:

IV. God has created us all, so we all need to regard each other with the same care and respect, which means treating individuals with disabilities in your families and communities with the same care and respect as non-disabled people.

V. People with disabilities are to be valued, even though they have various physical or mental limitations.

VI. The audience was encouraged to help the disabled in their personal, educational, and physical aspects of life. Included in this were children with disabilities. Children with disabilities should be given the same opportunities as nondisabled children, especially regarding education, though they may function at a lower level or learn at a slower pace.

VII.It is the responsibility of the adults to teach the non-disabled children to treat the disabled children with love, respect and kindness.

VIII.   Do not assume that children with disabilities are unable to lead successful and productive lives. If we do not support our children, whether disabled or non-disabled, they will not succeed or become a productive part of society.

Appendix C: New Delhi

Introduction to New Delhi

http://www.mapsofindia.com/delhi/population-of-new-delhi.html

http://delhitourism.nic.in/delhitourism/aboutus/index.jsp

http://www.tripadvisor.com/Travel-g304551-s303/New-Delhi:India:Public.Transportation.html

http://www.webindia123.com/territories/Delhi/Economy/Economy.htm

http://www.worldbank.org.in/WBSITE/EXTERNAL/COUNTRIES/SOUTHASIAEXT/INDIAEXTN/0,,contentMDK:21557057~pagePK:1497618~piPK:217854~theSitePK:295584,00.html

Summary of Joy's talk: Four Eternal Truths

I started with the Biblical story of Abraham and Isaac. I called my message "Four Eternal Truths," using the Scriptures from Genesis 22: 1-14 (The Holy Bible NIV), where Abraham was asked by God to sacrifice his only son, Isaac. All of God's promises to Abraham and his future generation depended on his son, Isaac.

Four points to the lesson:

• God asked Abraham to sacrifice his son as a burnt offering.

It was a temporary situation, which was a dark time in Abraham's life. God was testing Abraham to see how much he trusted God on the basis of what he had experienced and learned in the past about God. During the hard times, we need to remember the Truths about the Lord that we have learned in easier times.

• Our Spiritual journey is a walk of faith, not of feeling.

We can be obedient to God's commands, only when we can put our full trust in Him. In obedience to God, Abraham took the journey of faith to sacrifice Isaac. Before Abraham could even see the place where he was going to set up the altar, he told his servants to wait, "my son and I will go to worship God and we will be back." By faith Abraham knew that he would return with his son.

• When we walk by faith, God's promises always outnumber His commands.

If we have learned about God's promises from the Bible, we will know and experience that His promises and His blessings are much more than what He demands of us.

• Listen, for God will speak in a new way.

As Abraham was ready to sacrifice his son in obedience, he exhibited faith, and his ears were tuned in to God's voice, and at that point, "[11] But the Angel of the LORD called to him from heaven and said, "Abraham, Abraham!" So he said, "Here I am."

[12] And he said, "Do not lay your hand on the lad, or do anything to him; for now I know that you fear God, since you have not withheld your son, your only son, from me."

[13] Then Abraham lifted his eyes and looked, and there behind him was a ram caught in a thicket by its horns. So Abraham went and took the ram, and offered it up for a burnt offering instead of his son."

If Abraham's ears had not been tuned in to God's voice, he would not have heard God's message through the angel and would have done something God never intended.

At this point, I shared a dark time in my life: As a child, polio had paralyzed my body from my shoulders down to my feet, and at the time doctors had not given my parents any hope. They predicted that I would not live beyond five years, and if I lived, I would be in a vegetative state for the rest of my life. One doctor said that he could not bring life into a dead thing. After going to several doctors, my parents returned home and decided to pray, fast, and trust in God's promises, which they had learned in the light of His truth. My parents were walking by faith and not in the feelings of this world. After two weeks of my dad's fasting and praying, I wiggled one little toe. That was the beginning of God's answer to their prayers.

From that point on, I continued to slowly improve. I have often wondered why God did not heal me completely. When I chose to work in the disability field, I realized why–that my own disability helped me to understand disability and its implications a bit better. When we walk by faith, God's promises always outnumber his commands.

At the end of my talk, I challenged the ladies to continue to pray and encourage the people with disabilities, to provide others an understanding about disability, and to help the people with disabilities in whatever way they could. If we tune our ears to God, then he will speak His will for us in new ways.

Appendix D: Hubli

Introduction:

htttp://www.hubli.stpi.in/about.html

http://www.britannica.com/EBchecked/topic/274616/Hubli

http://www.encyclopedia.com/doc/1E1-HubliDha.html

http://www.tourism-of-india.com/karnataka-tour/hubli-tour.html

http://en.wikipedia.org/wiki/Hubli

http://stevens.usc.edu/pdf/hubli_dharwad.pdf?phpMyAdmin=Vw6
SrfJQHZk3o8%2CNjJbcUBQ13d9&phpMyAdmin=32cc4c658995t3
dd13768

http://www.equipindia.org/index.php?page=index

Power Points of Disability Ministry Training Seminars

Early Intervention

Early Intervention

Important Factors to Consider

By Karen A. Aukland, PT, PCS

March 2010 Revision

Importance of Early Intervention

- Brain Growth Spurts.
  - Occur frequently through 1st 3 years of life
  - Occur less frequently through childhood.
- Special activities during brain growth times
  - Increases potential for healing of damage
  - Can speed up normal development
- Waiting too long
  - Increases time needed to learn
  - Can Limit amount able to be learned

Diagnostics are Available to Identify Early Intervention Needs in Government Services

- But what can be done for Families that do not take advantage of this?
  - Parent/Family interviews (General Movement, Vision, Hearing)
- What about needs not currently included in Government Services?

Factors that Confuse Diagnosis of more Complex Developmental Concerns

- Sleep Issues
  - How much?
  - Snoring
- Tantrums
  - What causes them?
  - Frequency

Communication Skill - Short Summary of Development

- Crying
- Making sounds
- Repeating sounds
- Pointing for wants (10-12 months)
- Repeating words
- First words (1 to 1.5 years)
- Verbal turn taking (1 to 1.5 years)
- Repeating words to answer questions (2-3 years)
- Using 2 words together (2 years)
- Using 3 words together (3 years)
- Incorrect grammar
- Correct grammar (5 years)

Fine Motor – Short Summary of Development

- Laying on Back
  - Hands together – holding each other 3-4 months
  - Reaching – 3 months, Reach and grasp items – 5-6 months
- Laying On stomach
  - Pushing up on hands – 4-5 months (if baby has tummy time)
  - Reaching – 5 months, starting to work on grasping.
- Grasp
  - Reflexive to 3 months then working on control
  - Well controlled by 9 months
  - Pinch grasp emerges 9-12 months
- Functional Hand Use
  - Intent – 4 months
  - Object permanence – 7 months
  - Poking with index finger - 10 months
  - Using 2 hands together - 12 months

Gross Motor

- Head upright (when carried upright, on stomach)
- Sitting
- Crawling
- Standing
- Walking

Behaviors of Concern Autism Spectrum Disorders

- The presence of behaviors do not always indicate Autism Spectrum Disorders
- Behaviors indicate need for specific interventions to encourage learning

Behaviors of Concern Autism Spectrum Disorders

- Difference in quality/style of spoken language and body language
  - Interpreting facial expression/other gestures
  - Eye contact
  - Communication
    - Imitation of speech - Too much or Unable
    - Loss of Language
    - Talking self through activities
    - Tone/volume
    - Comprehension

Behaviors of Concern Autism Spectrum Disorders

- Restricted/Repetitive/Unusual/Limited Interests, Activities and Topics of Conversation
  - Atypical ways of doing things
  - Strong need for Routines/Rituals
  - Unusual reactions to events, people, objects
    - Excessive attachment or avoiding
    - Difficulty dealing with non-preferred
    - Difficulty sharing
  - Sensory Integration Issues
    - Foods – Color, Texture, Variety
    - Excessive need or avoidance of sensation (touch, body movement, etc.)

Behaviors of Concern
Autism Spectrum Disorders

◆ Differences in quality/style of social interactions
- Joining games
- Getting attention
- Using adults as tools
- Social conversation
- Lack of interest in others
- Needs one on one teaching to learn social rules
- Predicting intent and behavior of others.

Resources - Brain Growth

http://ecs.org/html/issue.asp?issueid=17

General Information

http://www.wisspd.org/htm/ATPracGuides/Training/ProgMaterials/CH980-09/BDCA.pdf

http://www.childdevelopmentinfo.com/development/piaget.shtml

http://main.zerotothree.org/site/DocServer/startingsmart.pdf?docID=2422

http://nccic.acf.hhs.gov/poptopics/brain.html

http://www.nea.org/home/31627.htm

Resources - Sleep and Tantrums

http://www.webmd.com/parenting/guide/sleep-children

http://www.sleepdex.org/deficit.htm

http://www.nasponline.org/resources/behavior/tantrums_ho.aspx

Resources - Gross Motor, Fine Motor, Communication

http://www.who.int/childgrowth/standards/motor_milestones/en/index.html (Gross Motor)

http://www.asha.org/public/speech/development/ (Speech and Language)

General Information

http://www.cdc.gov/ncbddd/actearly/milestones/

http://www.med.umich.edu/yourchild/topics/devmile.htm

Resources - Autism

http://www.asdatoz.com/Documents/Website-%20Some%20Information%20about%20Autism%20Spectrum%20Disorders%20trhd.pdf

General Information:

http://www.asdatoz.com/info.html

http://www.ninds.nih.gov/disorders/autism/detail_autism.htm

http://www.autism-society.org/

http://www.autism.com/

http://www.autismspeaks.org/what-autism

Learning Disability

Isaiah 9:2 (NKJV)

The people who walked in darkness

Have seen a great light;

Those who dwelt in the land of the shadow of death,

Upon them a light has shined.

Where are the People?

⊃ In your family
⊃ In your churches
⊃ In your neighborhood
⊃ In your community

What are they Like?

⊃ Like you and me
⊃ We have abilities
⊃ We also lack abilities

Abilities are like Members of our bodies
⊃ We all have members of our bodies
⊃ Some of us do not have the same members as others

Abilities & Members

⊃ When we obviously lack abilities (in the context of English)
 • The word Disability is used

⊃ When we lack members of our body (in the context of Hindi)
 • The word viklank is used

Abilities and Body Members Quickly and Easily Seen

⊃ Legs and Feet
⊃ Arms and Hands
⊃ Skin
⊃ Eyes
⊃ How we use them
 • Much
 • Little

⊃ You are all familiar with this because of the population you work with

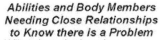

Abilities and Body Members Needing Close Relationships to Know there is a Problem

⊃ Ability to hear what is spoken
⊃ Ability to speak
⊃ Ability to understand what is spoken
⊃ Ability to use language to express
 • wants,
 • needs,
 • knowledge
⊃ In your families – are there adults or children with such difficulties?
⊃ In your neighborhoods? Villages?
⊃ Do you think they learn?

Abilities and Members Needing Close Relationships to Know there is a Problem

⊃ Ability or capacity to learn
  - Easy
  - Hard or Needing Help
⊃ Ability to remember what is learned
⊃ Ability to use what is learned in many ways

⊃ Some Labels:
  - Gifted
  - Mentally Retarded
  - Learning Disability

Abilities and Members Needing Help to Learn

⊃ What is Mental Retardation?
  - Limited **capacity or ability** to learn

⊃ What is Learning Disability?
  - Difficulty learning academic skills when **capacity or ability to learn is average**
  - Difficulty learning skills needed for success at school or work
  - A group of problems that may look like Mental Retardation – **but** they are NOT!

⊃ Have you grown up with children like this?

⊃ Can they learn?

Abilities and Body Members Needing Help to Learn

⊃ Learning Disabilities Impact Ability
  - Processing Written Language – Dyslexia
  - Processing Mathematics – Dyscalculia
  - Processing Handwriting – Dysgraphia
  - Processing Movement – Dyspraxia
  - Interpreting what is Heard – Auditory Processing
  - Interpreting what is Seen – Visual Processing

⊃ Think about a tube light
  - Power (special teaching) is given to the light – but nothing happens
  - Finally after a time with continuing power the light goes on
⊃ Do you know adults/children like this?

Abilities and Members Needing Help to Learn

⊃ Other Learning Problems
  - Attention or Focus
  - Ability to connect past experience with present actions
    - planning,
    - organizing,
    - managing time
    - managing space,
    - memory

Why Learning Disabilities?

⊃ Think of the Nerves in the Body and Brain as Roads.
⊃ Think of nerve signals traveling the roads as Lorries
⊃ At Villages and in Cities,
  - roads connect with other roads,
  - like nerves connect with other nerves

Why Learning Disabilities?

⊃ Lorries Slow Down or Stop Temporarily
  - Speed Bumps
  - Traffic
  - Bricks or dirt dumped in the road
  - Repairs

⊃ Lorries Detour Temporarily or Permanently
  - Individual Roads are so damaged they cannot be driven on until
    - repaired or
    - replaced by other roads
  - Festivals, Demonstrations, Parades
  - Some detours are long and involve more roads

⊃ BUT they still have Capacity to work

Learning Styles

◌ Sometimes a change in teaching approach is needed based on learning style
- Listening (Auditory)
- Looking (Visual)
- Using the body - hands/arms/feet/legs (Kinesthetic)

◌ Frequently more repetition is needed
◌ At times things can be remembered one day, but not the next.

Multiple Intelligences

◌ Sometimes Adapting Teaching to Use a Student's Strongest Ability is needed
- Body Movement – Kinesthetic
- Logical – Mathematical
- Interpersonal (with more than one person)
- Intrapersonal (alone)
- Visual Spatial
- Verbal (Spoken) – Linguistic
- Musical Rhythmic
- Naturalistic (Natural Environment)

Conditions that Imitate Learning Disabilities or Cause Behaviors that Interfere with Learning and Performance

◌ Lack of Sleep - Why?
- Personal Self-discipline or Lack of Parental Guidance.
- Psychiatric Issues such as Depression
- Sleep Apnea-breathing is blocked periodically during the night – more than 5 times per hour.
  - Sometimes Characterized by snoring, gasping for breath
  - Multiple Causes: Low muscle tone, enlarged tonsils, etc.
◌ Illnesses – Temporary and Chronic
◌ Stress!

Conditions that Imitate Learning Disabilities or Cause Behaviors that Interfere with Learning and Performance

◌ Decision Making When Under Stress
◌ Stress is not a situation, it is a person's response to a situation.

◌ When a person responds with stress, whether aware of it or not:

- 1. Risky alternatives will likely be chosen over safer, more reasonable alternatives.

Conditions that Imitate Learning Disabilities or Cause Behaviors that Interfere with Learning and Performance

- 2. Ability to understand what is being said by others decreases. There is less alertness to:

- a. determine/understand the most important thing being communicated by another person.

- b. read another person's body language or communication problem (i.e.discomfort, hostility, whispers of dangerous behavior)

Conditions that Imitate Learning Disabilities or Cause Behaviors that Interfere with Learning and Performance

- 3. Decreased ability to handle difficult tasks requiring focused attention (-- i.e. grief, other problem solving.

- 4. Difficulty remembering

- 5. Increased tendency to make choices prematurely instead of thinking things through.

Conditions that Imitate Learning Disabilities or Cause Behaviors that Interfere with Learning and Performance

- 6. Tolerating "ambiguity" (uncertainty, doubtfulness)

- 7. Decreased productive thinking and increased distractibility (taking on more things)

- 8. Distortion in perception of threat (positive & neutral events are interpreted negatively) which results in poor judgment. Tolerate and understand joking/sarcasm poorly.

Conditions that Imitate Learning Disabilities or Cause Behaviors that Interfere with Learning and Performance

- 9. When a "crisis" arouses fear/ frustration/ hostility then there is a greater tendency to use aggression and escape behaviors.

- 10. When stress occurs the only goals addressed are immediate survival goals. This means that long range goals are sacrificed.

⊃ NOTE: One of the highest forms of stress is guilt whether real or false.

Conditions that Imitate Learning Disabilities or Cause Behaviors that Interfere with Learning and Performance

⊃ POSITIVE ACTIONS IN DEALING WITH STRESS::

⊃ 1. Make Important Decisions Before Stress Occurs

⊃ 2. Determine Areas of Need and Develop a Plan when Calm

⊃ Decision Making Under Stress, from a Lecture by Wesley E. Sime, PhD/MPH/PhD Professor, Dept of Health & Human Performance University of Nebraska, Lincoln

Planning Instructional Strategies

⊃ Is the student learning with traditional teaching methods?
⊃ Do other teaching methods work better to help the student learn? - What are they?
⊃ Will the student need different materials than others to learn? (for example: Adapted materials – Bigger, simplified, assistive technology)

Planning Instructional Strategies

⊃ Will the curriculum need to be adapted? (Limiting amount to be learned, Changing how it is taught)
⊃ Will the sequence of teaching need to be changed? (First, Second)
⊃ Does the student need more personal assistance to learn? (Teacher, Other Students, Tutoring)?

125

Instructional Supports

ↄ Assistive Technology
ↄ Adaptations - Anything that helps someone learn
- Pictures
- Check lists and Task lists
- Calendars
- Reminders
- Word Lists
- Books

ↄ Adaptive Equipment
- Placement of Work (Slant board, Table, etc.)
- Seating Supports
- Special Teaching on how to Use Equipment

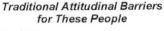

Traditional Attitudinal Barriers for These People

ↄ Disrespect
- Ignoring Needs
- Treating them as though they
  - Have less value
  - Are deliberately not trying
  - As though they are less able

ↄ When Disrespect is Present There is even Greater Risk for Worse Things to Happen!

Traditional Attitudinal Barriers for These People

ↄ Persecution

ↄ Emotionally – Abusing them by
- Mocking, Making Fun, Name Calling in general
- Impatience with their limitations
- Telling them they are stupid or stubborn
- Scolding for something they cannot change without help
- Other Disrespectful attitudes

ↄ Physically – Abusing them by Punishing
- For something they are unable to do without help
- For something they have not been given proper teaching to learn

Spiritual Consequences of Barriers

ↄ People who are hidden from the Light of God by isolation, by attitudes of disrespect and impatience being ignored or persecuted and driven away
- No opportunity to see the Light if they have not been shown in a way that they can understand
- No opportunity to hear about the Light if they have not been taught in a way that they can understand

Spiritual Consequences of Barriers

ↄ And... No opportunity to experience the respect and honor that Jesus would have given them
- if the followers of Christ do not show it to them
- If they are considered "less honorable", a curse, to be ashamed of....

Spiritual Consequences of Barriers

ↄ The Word Tells us of their Importance

- No, much rather, those members of the body which seem to be weaker are necessary. 1 Corinthians 12:22 (NKJV))

ↄ And... The Word Commands us

- And those members of the body which we think to be less honorable, on these we bestow greater honor; and our unpresentable parts have greater modesty. 1 Corinthians 12:23 (NKJV))

Remember what the Word Says

No, much rather, those members of the body
which seem to be weaker are necessary
1 Corinthians 12:22 (NKJV)

God Commands us regarding them 1
Corinthians 12:23a (NKJV)

- And those members of the body which we think to
  be less honorable, on these we bestow greater
  honor...

Isaiah 9:2 (NKJV)

The people who walked in darkness

Have seen a great light;

Those who dwelt in the land of the
shadow of death,

Upon them a light has shined.

Appendix E: Mundgod

http://en.wikipedia.org/wiki/Mundgod

http://www.binoygupta.com/travel_india/travel-india-mundgod-mini-tibet-54/

http://www.tibetsun.com/features/2008/12/23/mundgods-my-very-own-little-tibet/

Appendix F: Disability Ministry Training in 3 Districts by OEI

Sagar:

http://en.wikipedia.org/wiki/Sagara,_Karnataka

http://www.holidayiq.com/destinations/Sagar-Overview-3500.html

Davangere:

http://blog.indicorps.org/fellowship/gouri-tawady-learning-disability-awareness-campaign/

http://en.wikipedia.org/wiki/Davangere

http://www.tourism-of-india.com/karnataka-tour/davangere-tour.html

http://www.hindu.com/2009/04/12/stories/2009041254450400.htm

Chitradurga:

http://www.chitradurga.nic.in/history.html

http://www.southindiaonline.com/karnataka/chitradurga.htm

http://www.karnatakaholidays.com/chitradurga.php

http://en.wikipedia.org/wiki/Chitradurga_district

The topics and materials used in the training at Sagar, Davangere and Chitradurga are on the following pages.

Understanding Disability

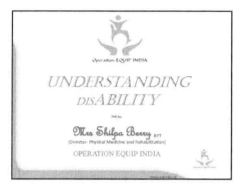

UNDERSTANDING
disABILITY

Mrs Shilpa Berry BPT
(Director- Physical Medicine and Rehabilitation)

OPERATION EQUIP INDIA

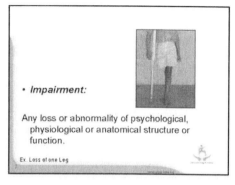

• *Impairment:*

Any loss or abnormality of psychological, physiological or anatomical structure or function.

Ex. Loss of one Leg

• *Disability:*

Any restriction or lack of ability to perform an activity in the manner or within the range considered normal for a human being.

Handicap:

A disadvantage for a given individual, resulting from an impairment or disability, that limits or prevents the fulfillment of a role that is normal, depending on the age, sex, social and cultural factors, for that individual.

CAUSES OF DISABILITY (GENERAL)

- Poor Nutrition during Pregnancy
- Genetic Factors
- Infectious Diseases
- Poor Sanitation
- Malnutrition
- Lack of Health and Rehabilitation Services
- Lack of Immunization
- Inappropriate Medicines used during Pregnancy
- Road Traffic Accidents
- Aging

DEFINING DISABILITY

According to the *Persons With Disability* (PWD) Act:

Disability Means:
- Blindness
- Low Vision
- Leprosy-cured
- Hearing Impaired
- Locomotion Disability (physical disability)
- Mental Retardation &
- Mental Illness

BLINDNESS

Blindness refers to a condition where a person suffers from any of the following conditions namely:

Poor Nutrition during Pregnancy

- Total absence of sight
- Visual Acuity not exceeding 6/60 (Snellen) in the better eye with correcting lenses
- Limitation of the field of vision subtending an angle of 20 degree or worse

LOW VISION

Person with low vision means a *person with impairment of visual functioning even after treatment* or standard refractive correction but who uses or is potentially capable of using vision for the planning or execution of a task with appropriate assertive devices.

LEPROSY CURED

"Leprosy cured person" means any person who has been cured of leprosy but is suffering from:

- Loss of sensation in hands or feet as well as loss of sensation and paresis in the eye and eyelid but with no manifest deformity.
- Manifest deformity and paresis but having sufficient mobility in their hands and feet to enable them to engage in normal economic activity.
- Extreme physical deformity as well as advanced age which prevents him from undertaking any gainful occupation.

HEARING IMPAIRMENT

"Hearing impairment" means loss of sixty decibels or more in the better ear in the conversational range of frequencies.

MENTAL RETARDATION

" Mental Retardation means a condition of arrested or incomplete development of mind of a person which is specially characterized by sub normality of intelligence.

MENTAL ILLNESS

Mental Illness means any mental disorder other than mental retardation

LOCOMOTION DISABILITY

"Locomotion disability" means disability of the bones, joints or muscles leading to substantial restriction of the limbs or any form of cerebral palsy.

"cerebral palsy" means a group of non-progressive conditions of a person characterized by abnormal motor control posture resulting from brain insult or injuries occurring in the pre-natal, peri-natal or infant period of development;

PHYSICAL DISABILITY

Common Diseases in India leading to Physical Disability:

- Post Polio Paralysis
- Brain Paralysis
- Club Foot (Congenital Talipes Equionovarus - CTEV)
- Rickets
- Epilepsy

POLIO

- Post Polio Residual Paralysis (PPRP)
- *Affects children aged 5 and below*
- *Stages of Polio*
- *Affects spinal Cord and Nerves*
- *Prevention- The only Cure.*
- *Typical features of PPRP*

BRAIN PARALYSIS

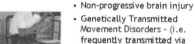

- Non-progressive brain injury
- Genetically Transmitted Movement Disorders - (i.e. frequently transmitted via Consanguineous marriages)
- Physical problems can be treated
- Secondary complications can be avoided

CLUB FEET

- Present at birth
- Early Diagnosis is the key

SERIAL CASTING AND SURGERY

131

RICKETS

- Vitamin D Deficiency
- Sunlight Exposure
- Deformities in Rickets

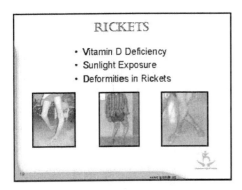

REHABILITATION

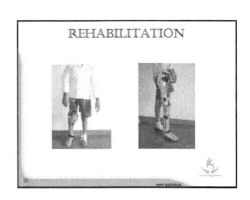

OTHER DISABILITIES NOT COVERED BY THE PERSONS WITH DISABILITIES ACT:

Autism

Autism, disorder that severely impairs development of a person's ability to communicate, interact with other people, and maintain normal contact with the outside world.

EPILEPSY

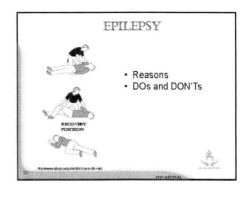

- Reasons
- DOs and DON'Ts

Social Stigma and Compassion

Anand Kumar Vanaparthy

Bible references are paraphrased or key parts quoted

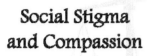

Stigma...

What is Stigma ?

- Stigma is a mark of social disgrace and the labelling of people as different (Meaning it is not caused by disease or situation, but is the result of people's attitudes)
- A distinguishing mark burned or cut into the flesh of a slave or criminal. It is a symbol of shame or mark of shame. It is derived from the word "stigmata" – bodily marks or pains (resembling the wounds of the crucified Christ)

Social Stigma ?

- In **John 9:2-3** Disciples asked Jesus "Master who sinned, this man or his parents, causing him to be born blind?" Jesus answered "Neither this man nor his parents"
- In **Luke 5:30** Pharisees asked Jesus "Why do you eat and drink with tax collectors and sinners" Who is being labeled as sinners?
- In **John 5:9** The woman of Samaria asked Jesus "Jews have no dealings with Samaritans" Why?
- In **John 8** The Pharisees brought a women caught in the act of adultery to Jesus. What is their intention?

- Helen Keller was blind, deaf and mute yet traveled the world advocating for the blind. She said:

- *"My problem is not my disability, but the attitude of the people towards my disability"*

Does stigma exist in our church and society?

Why?

- Why do beggars sit outside the Church?

- Why do some people in churches go to worship in church, but do not address the needs of beggars outside the church

- How many people affected with diseases/disabilities are included in our churches? If not...

Why?

People will show pity
but
not compassion

- There are many people affected with disabilities in India, but how many Christian ministries are committed to serve them?

Why?

- People choose a safe zone

- but not a risk zone

Reasons

- From the beginning – History says many people and groups are stigmatized for different reasons or circumstances (i.e. lepers, disabled, slaves, women, low caste people, Christians and people of other Faiths).
- Lack of Knowledge about these diseases (i.e. Belief that HIV/AIDS is a related to homosexual behavior, drug users or very promiscuous people. People do not want to associate with people living with HIV/AIDS because of these judgments.)

Reasons

- Their beliefs - Disease is a punishment or curse from their god
- Fears of contracting the disease through regular social contact
- Rejection of people living with disease
- Lack of passion and burden for persons with disability or disease

Consequences of Stigma

A SMUDGE

According to the Oxford dictionary SMUDGE means

"a blurred or smeared mark on the surface of something; an indistinct or blurred view or image."

13

Consequences of Stigma

- Discrimination, exclusion and isolation from families and communities
- Limited social interaction within the community
- Limited rights for children and adults with disease or disability

14

Consequences of Stigma

- Resources are not adequately prioritized because of the belief those persons are going to die anyway
- Can cause loss of employment if the health status of the employee is known
- Girls more than Boys are not provided the opportunity for education
- Lack of needed emotional and spiritual support

15

- **Barriers support stigma**

- **Jesus response was to break barriers and remove stigma**

16

1. Barriers for people with Disabilities

- Leviticus 21:16-22 (people were not allowed in to the temple for worship)
  BUT
- In Matt: 21:14 – Jesus healed the blind and lame people in the temple

- In Matt: 9:2 – Jesus forgives the sins of a man with paralysis

- In Matt: 20:34 – Jesus' shows compassion on a man with blindness

17

2. Barriers for people with Leprosy

- Leviticus13:43,44 – Leprosy made a person unclean in the Old Testament
  BUT
- In Mark 14:3 – Jesus sat and ate with a man who had leprosy in his house – Practical fellowship
- In Mark 1:41 – Jesus was moved with Compassion and stretch-out His hands and touched him and said to him "…..show yourself to the priest, and offer what Moses commanded" (In those days lepers were not allowed into the temple or permitted to give any offering)

18

2. Barriers of race, gender and culture

- Matthew 9:10-11 While Jesus was having dinner at Matthew's house, many tax collectors and sinners came and ate with him and his disciples. When the Pharisees saw this, they asked his disciples, "Why does your teacher eat with tax collectors and sinners?"

- Jesus crossed social barriers
  - John 4:7, 9 When a Samaritan woman came to draw water, Jesus said to her, "Will you give me a drink?" The Samaritan woman said to him, "You are a Jew and I am a Samaritan woman. How can you ask me for a drink?" (For Jews do not associate with Samaritans.)

19

2. Barriers with sexual sin

The Pharisees said, "Teacher, this woman was caught in the act of adultery. In the Law Moses commanded us to stone such women. Now what do you say?"

Jesus said, "Let any one of you who is without sin be the first to throw a stone at her."

At this, those who heard began to go away one at a time, the older ones first, until only Jesus was left, with the woman still standing there. Jesus straightened up and asked her, "Woman, where are they? Has no one condemned you?"

"No one, sir," she said.

"Then neither do I condemn you," Jesus declared. "Go now and leave your life of sin."

Jesus forgave her sin

20

Reactions Resulting from Stigma

21

22

1. Lack of **C**ompassion

2. Lack of **R**esponsibility

3. Lack of **O**bedience to fulfill great commission

4. Lack of **S**ervice

5. Lack of **S**pirituality

23

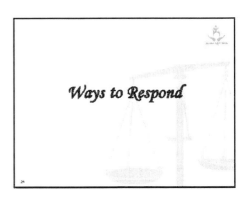

Ways to Respond

24

"If anyone desires to come after Me, let him deny himself, and take up his **Cross** daily, and follow Me"

Luke 9:23

Ministry – Act of Service

- "Ministry" from Christian perspective can be said to be an **Act of serving**
- Translation of word ministry
  - Kannada: Seve
  - Hindi: Seva
  - Marathi: Seva
  - Konkani: Seva
  - Telugu: Seva
- Seva is a concept of selfless service central to the Christian faith

---

1. Move with Love & Compassion

- Unconditional love - Loving even when behaviours are not pleasing
- Compassion – holding a sick person, loving your neighbour
- Caring without judgement - Separating the person from the behaviour and loving them for who they are
- Acknowledgement- Accepting and acknowledging the situation and taking action to assist.
- Grace- Acceptance of mistakes and sins without condemnation

---

- Jesus calls us to go and do the same for the sick and hurting in our communities

- Accept and share the love of Christ
  - "Whoever does not love does not know God, because God is love" 1 John 4:8

---

2. Have a Vision to Minister

- Extend trust and take responsibility
- In John 5:7 - The sick man answered Him "Sir I have no man to put me into the pool...."
  But
- In Luke 5:18 "men brought on a bed a man who was paralyzed..."

---

3. Reveal the secret of a purposeful life

Experiencing fullness of life

- "I cant walk properly. I didn't study much, since my school was very far from my residence. I was not able to enjoy my childhood as others do. People say, I am very good at making Handicrafts. So I took professional training at Equip India Rehabilitation centre. I am surprised to know that my artwork are being sold in Europe & America. Praise God! In my childhood, I was denied quality care at home, but today I am a successful worker. I know Jesus. I earn & support my family. After all, Disability is not inability". - young girl

31

Restored from misery to be a missionary!

- He was 63 years old. When he was 17 years old, he was affected by leprosy and was thrown out of his village. The disease worsened due to ignorance and deformed his hands and his feet.
- Being socially, physically and emotionally rejected by his family, friends and the community he went into depression and believed that it was a punishment from God for his Karma.
- But somehow he was directed to Indalga Leprosy hospital at Belgaum and started his treatment.
- After some years he was shifted to Hubli hospital for Handicapped, for further treatment. It was here that the Equip India team met him and with regular visitations and counseling shared about the love of Christ.
- He said "For the first time I had peace in my heart after hearing the message of Christ". The Love of Jesus has changed my life and has built my hopes and strengthened my faith."
- Even after his return to his village he received letters, literature and personal visitations that helped him to grow more spiritually. He was even connected to a local church where he received water Baptism.
- In the month of December 2009, he was invited to attend Blessing camp at the Equip India center. Being impressed with the teachings at the Camp, this man has made a decision to start a church in his village because "God has given me a burden "He says.

32

When Jesus saw the crowds, He had compassion on them, because they were harassed and helpless, like sheep without a Shepherd.

Matthew 9:36

1. **Vision**: Do we see what Jesus saw?

33

When Jesus saw the crowds, He was moved with compassion for them, because they were harassed and helpless, like sheep without a Shepherd.

Matthew 9:36

2. **Compassion** : Do you feel what Jesus felt?

34

Then He said to his disciples, ` The harvest is plentiful but the workers are few. So,( pray) Ask the Lord of the harvest, therefore, to send out workers into His harvest field`

Matthew 9:37

3. **Intercession:** Will we pray what Jesus asked?

35

" Jesus went through all the towns and villages, teaching in their synagogues, preaching the good news of the kingdom and healing every disease and sickness"

Matthew 9:35

4. **Transformation**: Will we do what Jesus did?

36

Henry Ford

- Coming together is beginning
- Staying together is progress
- Working together is success

HIV/AIDS Awareness

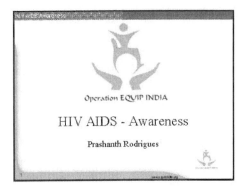

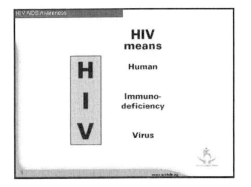

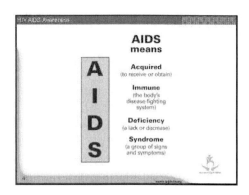

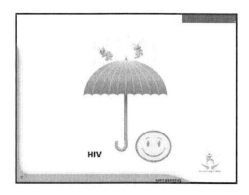

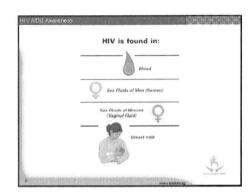

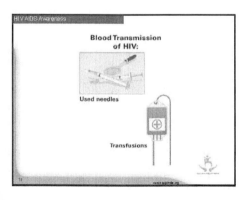

141

Ministry to People Living with Disabilities and HIV/AIDS

Ministry to People Living with Disabilities, Leprosy and HIV/AIDS

Challenges and Needs

Lilly Kanthi

- Objective
  - Why do we do this?
- Pretest
- Present Scenario
- Disability In India
- Challenges of Persons with Disability
- HIV/AIDS in India
- Challenges of Persons Living With HIV/AIDS
- Stigma
  - What is Stigma?
  - Why does Stigma exist?
  - Consequences of Stigma

Our knowledge decides our attitude

and

Our attitude decides our behavior

Why do we do this?

The Biblical Mandate is given in
Matthew 28:18-19 and Luke 14:13-14

The Great Commission and The Great Commandment mandate
that our first and foremost priority in all we do as Christians
is to bring all people *including those affected*
by disability, leprosy and HIV/AIDS
to a saving knowledge of Jesus Christ.

Pre- test

What do you feel or think when you
meet a person with
a Disability, Leprosy or HIV/AIDS?

- Feel pity?
- Feel uncomfortable?
- Feel ashamed to associate with them?
- Think it is a curse?

Leprosy ...

a) is dirty disease   b) is a curse   c) makes all lepers beggars

HIV/AIDS ...

a) is a result of sexual sin   b) leads to death

Persons with Disabilities ...

a) are a burden to the family b) are always dependant

c) make me feel uncomfortable because I don't know much about
them / I don't know how to deal with them

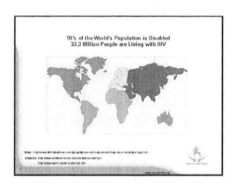

10% of the World's Population is Disabled
33.3 Million People are Living with HIV

Disability In India
2.1% of Population is Physically Disabled
21.9 million
•Accidents
•Polio
•Correctible
•Leprosy
•Deformities

47% of persons with diabilities *never* marry

Only 9% finish secondary school

74% of persons with disabilities are unemployed

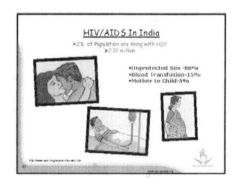

HIV/AIDS In India
>2% of Population are living with HIV
>2.31 million
•Unprotected Sex ~80%
•Blood Transfusion-15%
•Mother to Child-5%

Scenario of HIV/AIDS in the World

- 38.6 Million people are infected with HIV/AIDS*

- 11 Million are youth between the age of 15-24

- 15 Million children have lost their parents

- 30 Million people have lost their lives.

Challenges for People with Disabilities, Leprosy & HIV/AIDS
Lack of Rehabilitation
Lack of Special Ed.
Lack of Wheelchairs
Lack of Income
Lack of Knowledge of the Gospel

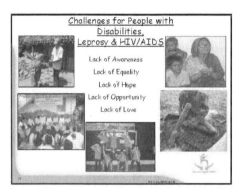

Barriers

Attitudinal Barriers:

- Background
- Knowledge

Physical Barriers

- Building and the physical environment of the church, homes, and community
- Transportation Barriers
- Communication Barriers

Church Response to the Disability Community

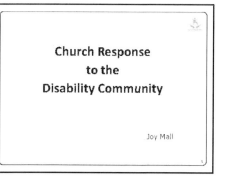

Church Response
to the
Disability Community

Joy Mall

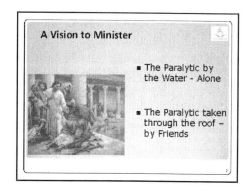

A Vision to Minister

- The Paralytic by the Water - Alone

- The Paralytic taken through the roof – by Friends

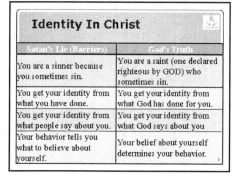

Ministry of Jesus

Jesus healed   (Physically, Spiritually)

Jesus comforted

Jesus fed

Jesus rebuked

Jesus taught

Jesus preached

Jesus made a way to heaven

All of that was ministry. Jesus spent his life helping others.

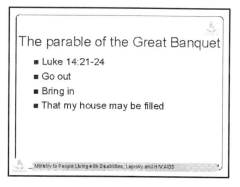

The parable of the Great Banquet

- Luke 14:21-24
- Go out
- Bring in
- That my house may be filled

Ministry to People Living with Disabilities, Leprosy and HIV/AIDS

Identity In Christ

Satan's Lie (Barriers)	God's Truth
You are a sinner because you sometimes sin.	You are a saint (one declared righteous by GOD) who sometimes sin.
You get your identity from what you have done.	You get your identity from what God has done for you.
You get your identity from what people say about you.	You get your identity from what God says about you
Your behavior tells you what to believe about yourself.	Your belief about yourself determines your behavior.

Because there is freedom of soul in the Truth

www.squidoo.org

Where can you find persons affected with Disabilities?

WAYS TO RESPOND
Find the People with Disabilities

- In the church
- Right outside the church
- In the neighborhoods
- In the village
- In the homes you know about

WAYS TO RESPOND
Find the People with Disabilities

- Visit orphanages
- Visit schools and colleges
- Visit homes for women
- Visit rehabilitation centers
- Visit hospitals
- Visit leper colonies
- Visit hospice locations

WAYS TO RESPOND
Find the People with Disabilities

- Search everywhere
  - In stations
  - Outside temples
  - Marketplace and shopping areas
  - At the sides of the streets
  - High ways and by ways

How to Identify Needs

- Emotional needs
  - Someone to listen
  - Someone to give advice
- Physical needs
  - Basic necessities (clothing, food, shelter)
  - Help to access available services

How to Identify Needs

- Spiritual needs
  - Prayer
  - Introduction to Jesus

- Mix with them and get their input

Identify Barriers based on Needs

- Assess barriers
  - Physical
  - Attitudinal
- Remove physical barriers
  - Install ramp
  - Fit guide rails
  - Accessible toilets
  - Attitude education

Remove attitude barriers

- Pastor and the church leaders should share the vision of Disability Ministry with the church
- Have someone share their testimony in the service from the group you have worked with or want to work with
- Conduct training, especially in the areas of HIV and leprosy - people need to know that it is safe to be around those with these diseases
- Avoid establishing different services for the target group - this only helps to keep the barriers in place

WAYS TO RESPOND
Do something which builds them

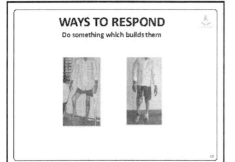

Experiencing Fullness of Life

She found the love of Christ

Through vocational training developed her God given gift

Today she is a successful worker.

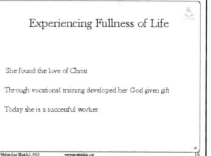

WAYS TO RESPOND
Do something which builds them up

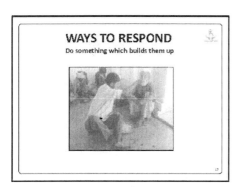

WAYS TO RESPOND

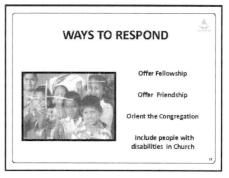

Offer Fellowship

Offer Friendship

Orient the Congregation

Include people with disabilities in Church

Inclusion in the Church is involvement

- Pray for them and with them
- Worship
- Sunday School
- Prayer Meeting/Bible Study
- Church Activities
- Social Activities

How to Include?

- Assess and Identify Barriers
- Remove Barriers
- Identify needs
- Response
- Case Studies

Response

- Identify the message you want to share
  - Hope for the future for them
  - Love of God demonstrated to them
  - Identify some small initial projects you can involve in to build up relationships
  - Fun camp
  - Health camp through OEI
  - Access to medical resource (surgery, rehabilitation)
  - Wheelchair distribution (through OEI and JAF)

WAYS TO RESPOND
Positive Network

a. Governmental Benefits and services
b. Non-Governmental Organization (NGO) service
c. Training centers (Vocational etc.)
d. Educational opportunities

How to Love people with Disabilities, Leprosy and HIV/AIDs

How does Christ show his love for the world?
He died for us. Greater love.....

Demonstrate your love in action.
We cannot minister to them unless we love them.

Testimony

- Normal child birth
- Polio at age 4 months
- Living with disability in India
- High School: Dedicated life to Lord Jesus
- 2000-Present: Disability Ministry

A Vision of Disability Ministry

Joy Mall

Impairment, Disability, and Handicap

- Impairment: Any loss of abnormality of psychological, physiological, or anatomical structure or function
- Disability: Any restriction or lack of ability to perform an activity in the manner or within the range considered normal for a human being
- Handicap: Disadvantage for a given individual, resulting from an impairment or disability, that limits or prevents the fulfillment of a role that is normal, depending on age, sex, social and cultural factors, for that individual.

Mandate for Disability Ministry

Luke 14:21b-23

...'Go out quickly into streets and alleys of the town and bring in the poor, the crippled, the blind and the lame.'

'Sir,' the servant said, 'what you ordered has been done, but there is still room'

Then the master told his servant, 'Go out to the roads and country lands and **make them come in,** so that my house will be full.'

Another translation says 'compel them to come, so that my house will be full.'

Church Ministry for People with Disabilities

- The reason the churches need disability ministry

Mark 16:15 NIV
He said, to them "Go into all the world and preach the good news to all creation."

- People with disabilities are part of **all creation.**

We Are Called...

To bring the good news to people with disabilities,
To bring the people with disabilities in to your churches,
To encourage the people with disabilities
And **to use** their God given gifts and talents for His glory.

Commitment and Vision

"Most of my clients desire to go to church but they cannot find churches that are accessible or a church where they feel welcome."

149

What is Disability Ministry?

- An activity of Christians with and without disabilities working together to reach people affected by disabilities by sharing the Gospel, to integrate them into the church, and to meet their needs in a way that serves as a witness to the surrounding community.

7

Ministry begins...

- Prayer
- Fasting

8

Purpose of the Church

- Inclusion!!!
  - Integrate the individual into the church body.
  - Train and prepare the church to welcome people with disabilities in a normal way that will make them feel comfortable.

9

Statistics

- 800,00 disabled people in Chicago
- 1,630,000 disabled people in U.S.
- 650 million disabled people worldwide

- 12,000 churches in Chicago area
  - Only 100 known to cater to disabled needs by Joni & Friends

10

3 Important Steps

- Evangelism
- Discipleship
- Prepare them for ministry

11

People with Disabilities need to hear about:

1.) God of love.
2.) God who gave His only son for us.
3.) God who forgives us form our sins and gives us eternal life.

12